## Also by Ric Edelman

*The Lies About Money*

*The Truth About Money*

*Ordinary People, Extraordinary Wealth*

*Discover the Wealth Within You*

*The New Rules of Money*

*What You Need to Do Now*

# RESCUE YOUR MONEY

from bad investments, as well as big losses, excessive fees, high taxes, and avoidable risks, caused by painful mistakes, major missteps, immense blunders, giant slip-ups, large gaffes, enormous oversights, whopping errors, second thoughts, cumbersome rationalizations, and wild guesses, all because you got bad advice, poor counsel, silly suggestions, errant recommendations, idiotic opinions, incorrect instructions, and useless information from know-nothing pundits, arrogant journalists, self-proclaimed experts, idea-of-the-day columnists, commission-seeking brokers, and inexperienced advisors, all of whom you thought were smart but who you now realize are actually ill-informed, uneducated, inexperienced, unskillful, untrained, flat-out wrong, or just plain stupid.

## Ric Edelman

*New York     London     Toronto     Sydney*

Free Press
A Division of Simon & Schuster, Inc.
1230 Avenue of the Americas
New York, NY 10020

First Free Press paperback edition March 2009

FREE PRESS and colophon are trademarks of Simon & Schuster, Inc.

For information about special discounts for bulk purchases, please contact Simon &
Schuster Special Sales at 1-800-456-6798 or business@simonandschuster.com.

The Simon & Schuster Speakers Bureau can bring authors to your live event. For more
information or to book an event contact the Simon & Schuster Speakers Bureau at
866-248-3049 or visit our website at www.simonspeakers.com.

Designed by Ric Edelman and Christine Janaske

Manufactured in the United States of America

20   19   18   17   16   15   14   13   12   11

Library of Congress Cataloging-in-Publication Data is available.

ISBN-13: 978-1-4391-5290-4
ISBN-10:      1-4391-5290-X

# NOTE TO READERS

This publication contains the opinions and ideas of its author. The strategies outlined in this book may not be suitable for every individual and are not guaranteed or warranted to produce any particular results. Presentation of performance data herein does not imply that similar results will be achieved in the future. Any such data is provided merely for illustrative and discussion purposes; rather than focusing on the time periods used or the results derived, the reader should focus instead on the underlying principles.

This book is sold with the understanding that neither publisher nor author, through this book, is engaged in rendering legal, tax, investment, insurance, financial, accounting, or other professional advice or services. If the reader requires such advice or services, a competent professional should be consulted. Relevant laws vary from state to state.

No warranty is made with respect to the accuracy or completeness of the information contained herein, and both the author and the publisher specifically disclaim any responsibility for any liability, loss, or risk, personal or otherwise, which is incurred as a consequence, directly or indirectly, of the use and application of any of the contents of this book.

This book is dedicated to the many frustrated, aggravated, irritated, annoyed, displeased, dismayed, shocked, and confused investors who, despite being worried, apprehensive, anxious, nervous, fearful, and frightened, are convinced that financial security and prosperity can and will be theirs, if someone will simply show them the way.

## Acknowledgments

In the Panic of 2008, the life savings of millions of Americans plunged in value. Now many are desperate to avoid further losses, while others fear that financial security is forever beyond their reach. As a result, consumers across the country are impulsively making bad investment decisions that will only worsen their predicament. They need solid and effective advice, and they need it fast.

That advice is in your hands, and it's being delivered to you in record time — just weeks from concept to bookstore shelves.

I am indebted to financial advisors James Baker, Alfonso Burgos, Scott Butera, Kristine Chaze, Isabel Cooper, Brandon Corso, Marty Corso, John Davis, Mary Davis, Patrick Day, Alan Facey, David Heinemann, Erich Hoffman, Diane Jensen, Jan Kowal, J.B. Liebstein, Andrew Massaro, Frances Martin, Ed Moore, Ken Murray, Helen Nichols, Betty O'Lear, Doug Rabil, Darrell Reynard, Rey Roy, Jennifer Sevier, Valentino Taddei, Christine Wessinger, Sean Wintz, Tom Wood, Anderson Wozny, and Tom Wright, and to contributors Mark Bagley, Duke Fanelli, Evy Sheehan, Kris Spadaccia, and Katie Tracy.

My gratitude goes to graphic designers Christine Janaske and Suzi Fenton, who masterfully designed the book. Many thanks, too, to Will Casserly, who oversaw and made major contributions during the creative process. He, along with Christine Janaske, also designed the book's front and back covers. Kelly Pike's many fine editorial suggestions helped in ways large and small.

I appreciate the efforts of my data go-to guy, Robert Bowman, and his team, Jeff Allen, Adam Epling, and Andrew Kramer, whose work is displayed in the book's many charts and graphs. Credit also goes to my executive assistant, Stacy Brosnahan, whose diligence ensured that I met everyone's deadlines.

Thanks go to Free Press for its willingness to rush this book to the market. I'm grateful to my editor, Dominick Anfuso, assistant editor Leah Miller, editorial assistant Sharbari Bose, copy editor Philip Bashe, associate publisher Suzanne Donahue, executive vice president and publisher Martha K. Levin, and the publicity team led by Carisa Hays and Nicole Kalian. And, as always, thanks to my agent, Gail Ross.

Most important is my wife, Jean. Her love and support make everything I do possible.

# Foreword

I am a retired Marine, and I teach a financial institutions and markets course for college students. Over the years, I have told my students to listen to Ric Edelman on the radio and read his books to learn more about investments. One year a student actually contacted Ric and had a series of phone conversations with him about her research topic, reverse mortgages. Ric patiently helped her, and I was not surprised.

Every now and then I encounter someone, maybe a workman or a plumber, who wants to know more about financial planning. I always tell them the same thing I tell my students: read Ric's classic, *The Truth About Money*. On several occasions I've given that book to a young person (or a not-so-young person who confesses he or she needs help in this area), and soon thereafter, I usually get a phone call telling me that the book was the easiest book they had ever read and that they were already putting into practice what they learned.

I have attended several of Ric's seminars over the years and have always enjoyed them. Ric loves making difficult concepts easy to understand for the average person. He has a ready wit and connects with the audience. He pokes fun at himself, enjoys a laugh, and makes you laugh, too.

I have heard him confess once or twice on his radio program that he may not know the answer to a caller's question, and then he would ask for a tax attorney, CPA, or other professional to call him at the studio. He's not afraid to admit when he doesn't have the answer, and that's why we know we can believe him when he offers advice.

Ric is a national treasure. He is one of the best examples of a person who is living his personal dream by helping others achieve theirs.

— Francis X. Bergmeister

*Instead of asking the publisher to find a celebrity for the foreword, Ric invited listeners of his nationally syndicated radio show to submit entries. A long-time listener, Frank holds the Certified Financial Planner™ certification and has served as the education director for the Certified Financial Planner Board of Standards, Inc. To see other finalists, go to RicEdelman.com.*

# *Contents*

**Overview**

The Secret to Successful Investing ...................................1

**Chapter 1**

One Major Goal You Should Have ....................................7

**Chapter 2**

The Two Major Obstacles That You'll Face .................. 11

*Obstacle 1:* Taxes ................................................................ 11

*Obstacle 2:* Inflation Erodes Your Buying Power.... 14

Why Those Who Invest "Safely" Often Go Broke.... 16

The Minimum Return You Must Earn ......................... 21

Investments That Can Generate the
Returns You Need........................................................... 23

**Chapter 3**

**One Big Question** ................................................................. 27

    Market Timing — aka Buy Low/Sell High ............... 28

    Following the Fads ............................................. 31

    Do You Trust the Media? .................................... 37

    Not-So-Expert Advice ........................................ 42

    Don't Count On Quality ..................................... 45

    Hot Sectors That Aren't ..................................... 50

**Chapter 4**

**The Two "Truths" That Prevent You from Investing Successfully**

**The Two "Truths" That Prevent You from Investing Successfully** ................................................ 55

    *Basic Truth 1:* Stock Prices Rise and Fall ............ 56

    *Basic Truth 2:* The Stock Market Is Risky, Volatile, and Unpredictable ................................. 60

    Why You Mustn't Look ....................................... 64

    The Truth About the Two Basic Truths ............... 65

    A Cautionary Tale ............................................. 69

**Chapter 5**

**The Secret** ............................................................... 75

    It's a Game of Horseshoes, Not a Horse Race ....... 82

    Something Else the Media Never Tell You ............ 83

    Optimizing Versus Maximizing ............................ 87

**Chapter 6**

**The Secret to the Secret** ...................................................... 93

*Crucial Step 1:* Maintain a Long-term Focus ............. 94

*Crucial Step 2:* Buy Low/Sell High .............................. 116

The Penalty If You Fail to Buy Low/Sell High ........ 124

The Right Time to Buy Low/Sell High ...................... 126

Rebalancing by Time ...................................................... 126

Rebalancing by Percentage .......................................... 127


**Chapter 7**

**What If You're Already Retired?** ..................................... 131


**Chapter 8**

**The Most Important Part of the Secret** ...................... 135

Turnover ............................................................................. 144

Fees ...................................................................................... 146


**Conclusion** ............................................................................. 157

**Ric's Recipe** ........................................................................... 160

**Notes** ........................................................................................ 161

**Index** ........................................................................................ 163

# *Overview: The Secret to Successful Investing*

What is the secret to successful investing? If you're like many Americans, you've sought the answer. Indeed, there's no shortage of ideas. Stocks, bonds, mutual funds, real estate, options trading, commodities — you've encountered dozens of ways to invest. You've also tried some of them.

And they've all led you to the same place: this book.

After all, if any of those ideas had made you rich, you wouldn't be reading this page right now.

> *"An investment in knowledge always pays the best interest."*

— *Benjamin Franklin*

I've seen a lot of people like you in my more than twenty years as a financial advisor. You're careful with your money, and you want to make it grow. You've tried a lot of ideas, maybe even worked with a broker or two (or three), but nothing seems to have worked.

That's okay. It's even common. Throughout the decades that my firm has been managing billions of dollars for people just like you, I've spent a lot of time studying investment strategies and learning how consumers get it wrong, and what you need to do to get it right.

And do I have exciting news for you: I've found the secret to successful investing, and I'm sharing it with you in this book. The secret is so clear, so obvious, and so easy that you'll kick yourself for missing it all these years. To find out what that secret is, all you have to do is turn the page.

# Buy Low

# Sell High

Uh-oh. I suspect you're feeling a little disappointed. Maybe even a little annoyed. *I paid how much for a book that tells me to buy low/sell high? You've got to be joking.*

Indeed, you are probably hoping — even assuming — that I *am* joking. Everyone knows that you're supposed to buy low/sell high. And everyone also knows the line is a joke, because everyone knows that it can't be done.

But it's really true. The key to investment success really *is* buying low and selling high. And in this book, I really am going to show you how to do it.

To help you understand how to do it correctly, I'm also going to show you:

☞ the one major goal you should have as you seek investment success;

☞ the two major obstacles that you'll encounter;

☞ one big question you'll have to face; and

☞ two basic "truths" that confront — and confound — every investor.

In the short time it takes you to finish this book (I bet you can read it cover to cover in one sitting), you'll know how to construct a portfolio that can provide you with above-average returns, below-average risks, and below-average costs.

So let's get started.

# *One Major Goal*
# *You Should Have*

When people seek investments, they tend to have one goal in mind: they want to beat the market.

Don't agree? Then tell me why you compare the performance of your investments with Standard & Poor's 500 Index. You're gauging your success by comparing your investment results with the overall market, as measured by the S&P 500, the Dow Jones Industrial Average, or some other index. If you're beating the market, you're happy. If you're not, you're unhappy.

Guess what? Trying to beat the market is the wrong goal.

In fact, that is a disastrous goal. Taking that approach sets you up for failure.

Why? It's really very simple. And we need look no further back than 2008 to find a perfect example. In 2008 the S&P 500 lost 38.5 percent.*[1] If you lost only 30 percent, congratulations! You beat the market!

Somehow I doubt that you (or your spouse) would be thrilled at such news.

Thus, we must remember that "beating the market" isn't the point. In fact, only one thing matters when it comes to investing: achieving financial security. *That* is your one major goal.

Think about it. The purpose of investing is to help you accomplish your goals, whether that means sending

*The sources for all statistics can be found on page 161.*

your kids to college, retiring comfortably, or caring for aging parents. It's financial security that matters, not some benchmark that has no relevance to your personal life.

People who focus on the market are missing the point. You need to emphasize your goals.

## 2

# *The Two Major Obstacles That You'll Face*

If financial security is the goal, you'll soon encounter a couple of problems. Let's explore them.

### *Obstacle 1: Taxes*

The first obstacle you'll encounter is taxes.

When you earn money from your occupation, you pay income taxes.

When you purchase goods, you pay sales taxes.

If you invest money, you'll pay income taxes on the interest you earn or capital gains taxes on the dividends and profits.

If you buy real estate (and in some jurisdictions, cars, boats, and airplanes), you'll pay property taxes.

If you give your money to family members, you (not them) might have to pay gift taxes.

And if you should die with more money than Congress feels is appropriate, your estate will pay estate taxes.

As everyone who has accumulated money knows, money does not solve every problem. But it sure does create new ones.

FIGURE 2.1

# Top Tax Rates
## as of January 1, 2009

*Federal Income Tax* **35%**

*Capital Gains Tax* **15%**

*Estate Tax* **45%**

*Gift Tax* **45%**

*Local Property Tax* **2.8%**

*State Sales Tax* **7.25%**

Sources: All data current as of January 1, 2009, and provided by Internal Revenue Service except for Local Property Tax data, which is provided by the 2005 American Community Survey, produced by the U.S. Census Bureau.

## *Obstacle 2: Inflation Erodes Your Buying Power*

The other obstacle to financial security is harder to notice (because you never actually write a check for it, like you do to the IRS), but it's just as damaging as taxes.

As shown in Figure 2.2, inflation has averaged 3.2 percent from 1926 through 2008. Sometimes it's higher, like from 1973 to 1974, when inflation averaged 8.6 percent. Other times it's quite low, as in 1998, when it was only 1.6 percent. But over long periods, it has been remarkably consistent at 3.2 percent.[2]

FIGURE 2.2

# Inflation Is a Fact of Life

*Since 2003* **3.2%**

*Since 1983* **3.2%**

*Since 1926* **3.2%**

CPI for All Urban Consumers. Source: Bureau of Labor Statistics.

## *Why Those Who Invest "Safely" Often Go Broke*

The sad truth is that taxes and inflation most hurt the people who know the least about investing.

Let's assume that you place $100,000 into a five-year bank certificate of deposit that pays 3.1 percent in interest annually. That's the average CD rate as of December 31, 2008, according to Bankrate.com.

If you earn 3.1 percent, you earn $3,100 in interest. Of course, you don't get to keep all that money because the interest is taxable.

Let's assume that you pay both federal and state income taxes. Let's further assume that your combined federal/state tax bracket is 30 percent. Since the CD paid 3.1 percent, you lose 0.93 percent to taxes, leaving you with a profit of 2.17 percent.

But let's not forget inflation. If inflation is averaging 3.2 percent, you're actually losing 1.03 percent on every dollar you invested in that CD. Now, losing

1.03 percent annually might not seem like much, considering that the S&P 500 lost 38.5 percent in 2008. But the stock market doesn't lose every year, while the CD does.

If you lose 1.03 percent every year for twenty years, guess what happens? You end up losing 20.6 percent of your money. In other words, if you start with $100,000, over twenty years you'll watch your money "grow" to $79,400 in real economic terms.

To understand the crisis this presents, consider the couple who both retire at age sixty-five. They've spent years — two full, lifelong careers — accumulating their savings, and they know that the money they currently have is all the money they will ever have. If they lose it, it's gone. They know that, unlike a thirty-year-old, they don't have another thirty-five years to regenerate their savings. So they invest carefully, choosing investments that can't lose money. They reject the stock market as too risky and instead place their life savings into bank CDs.

 FIGURE 2.3

## How Taxes and Inflation Affect You

| | |
|---|---|
| **Five-year CD** | **3.10%** |
| **30% Tax Rate** | **− 0.93%** |
| | **2.17%** |
| **Average Inflation** | **− 3.20%** |
| **Annual Result** | **− 1.03%** |
| | **x 20 yrs** |
| **20-year Result** | **− 20.60%** |

### $100,000 invested today would be worth only $79,400 in 20 years

Earnings reflect hypothetical return, not meant to reflect any specific investment. Taxes based on 30% combined federal/state income tax rate. Inflation rate is based on the average for the Consumer Price Index from 1926 through 2008 according to the Bureau of Labor Statistics. Past performance does not guarantee future results.

And for a while, they're fine. Between their pensions, Social Security, and the interest they earn from the CDs, they have an annual income that easily meets their needs. Everything seems fine.

But let's fast-forward. In twenty years, they will discover that their strategy has failed them. You see, at 3.2 percent annual inflation, the cost of living doubles every 23 years. But most pension checks (for those lucky enough to get them) don't increase. Nor do payments from annuities. Social Security checks notoriously rise only 1 or 2 percent per year, well below the average inflation rate. As a result, it takes twice as much income at age eighty-eight to buy the same goods and services that they used to buy at age sixty-five.

Indeed, everything seems fine and dandy at age sixty-five. But some twenty years later, money is tight. Do you know any retirees in their seventies, eighties, or nineties who say that they don't have as much money as they need? Chances are, they were fine financially twenty or so years ago.

If you limit yourself to investments that don't keep up with inflation, you'll find yourself in a serious financial predicament in the future. You'll discover that the cost of everything has doubled — but your income hasn't.

That's what happens when you plop the bulk of your money into low-yielding investments. You'll go broke, and you'll do it safely.

And that's the irony. The people who are putting their life savings into bank CDs do so because they want safety above all else. They don't want to put their money in the stock market because they fear losing money. They're afraid to invest in real estate. They don't understand international securities. So they choose bank accounts, which (they think) offer safe, predictable, and stable rates of return.

Predictable and stable, yes. Safe, no.

As a result, millions of Americans are going broke safely. And they don't even know it.

### *The Minimum Return You Must Earn*

This is why you must overcome the long-term impact of taxes and inflation.

To see exactly how much you must earn merely to *break even* relative to taxes and inflation, look at Figure 2.4 on the next page. It shows how much you must earn, based on your combined federal and state income tax bracket and the current rate of inflation.

For example, if inflation is 3 percent and you are in the 30 percent combined federal/state tax bracket, you must earn 4.3 percent just to break even. If your investments are earning less than that, you're losing money in real economic terms.

This leads to just one question: Where can you earn more than the minimum return indicated in Figure 2.4?

You won't do it by investing in bank checking or savings accounts, money market funds, bank CDs,

FIGURE 2.4

# Just to Break Even
### Here's the minimum return you must earn based on your tax bracket and inflation

| Combined Federal and State Tax Bracket | Inflation Rate | | | | |
|---|---|---|---|---|---|
| | 3% | 4% | 5% | 6% | 7% |
| 10% | 3.3% | 4.4% | 5.6% | 6.7% | 7.8% |
| 12.5% | 3.4% | 4.6% | 5.7% | 6.9% | 8.0% |
| 15.0% | 3.5% | 4.7% | 5.9% | 7.1% | 8.2% |
| 17.5% | 3.6% | 4.9% | 6.1% | 7.3% | 8.5% |
| 20.0% | 3.8% | 5.0% | 6.3% | 7.5% | 8.8% |
| 22.5% | 3.9% | 5.2% | 6.5% | 7.7% | 9.0% |
| 25.0% | 4.0% | 5.3% | 6.7% | 8.0% | 9.3% |
| 27.5% | 4.1% | 5.5% | 7.0% | 8.3% | 9.7% |
| 30.0% | 4.3% | 5.7% | 7.1% | 8.6% | 10.0% |
| 32.5% | 4.4% | 5.9% | 7.4% | 8.9% | 10.4% |
| 35.0% | 4.6% | 6.2% | 7.7% | 9.2% | 10.8% |
| 37.5% | 4.8% | 6.4% | 8.0% | 9.6% | 11.2% |
| 40.0% | 5.0% | 6.7% | 8.3% | 10.0% | 11.7% |
| 42.5% | 5.2% | 7.0% | 8.7% | 10.4% | 12.2% |
| 45.0% | 5.5% | 7.3% | 9.1% | 10.9% | 12.7% |
| 47.5% | 5.7% | 7.6% | 9.5% | 11.4% | 13.3% |
| 50.0% | 6.0% | 8.0% | 10.0% | 12.0% | 14.0% |

T-bills, government savings bonds, life insurance, or (for most people) in fixed annuities.

Despite this fact, millions of Americans have placed trillions of dollars into those investments. They wonder why they aren't able to keep pace with the cost of living, and they demand that Congress do something about it.

Too bad they don't realize that the solution is in their grasp. Fortunately, by reading this book, it's in yours.

Literally.

### *Investments That Can Generate the Returns You Need*

If putting all your money into bank accounts won't provide you with investment success, where can you generate the returns you need?

The answer is in Figure 2.5.

Over the past thirty years, each of the three major asset classes (stocks, bonds, and real estate) generated double-digit returns (or nearly so).

Sure, in any given year or couple of years, each of these asset classes has generated losses. But you're not investing for a year or two. You're investing for a lifetime, so it makes sense to focus on the average returns earned by a lifetime of investing.

FIGURE 2.5

## These Do Not Produce the Returns You Need

Checking Accounts

Savings Accounts

Money Market Funds

Bank CDs

Treasury Bills

EE Savings Bonds

Life Insurance Policies

Fixed Annuities

## These Can

*Average Annual Return 1979–2008*

| | |
|---|---|
| Bonds | *9.4%* |
| Real Estate | *10.3%* |
| U.S. Stocks | *11.0%* |

Data reflect the S&P 500 Stock Index, U.S. Long-term Corporate Bond Total Return Index, and NAREIT Total Return Index.
Source: Ibbotson Associates. Past performance does not guarantee future results.

# *One Big Question*

Okay, so now you know that you need to earn higher returns than those offered by bank accounts and the like.

You now have only one question: How do you earn those returns?

It's simple. And I've already told you the answer.

Buy low/sell high.

## *Market Timing — aka Buy Low/Sell High*

Of course, just about everyone who tries to buy low/ sell high fails at some point or other. That's because they do it wrong. Soon I'll show you how to do it correctly — every time. But first, let's explore how other people try to buy low/sell high. There's value in examining the mistakes of others.

First of all, the idea is tempting. For obvious reasons, a person who manages to always buy low/sell high will be immensely successful. That's why so many people try to do this. It also explains why the media constantly offer advice on what to buy, what to sell, and when to do it.

There's only one problem: such "market timing" advice is never correct on a consistent basis. As a result, the overwhelming majority of people who try to buy low/ sell high wind up getting it backward.

For proof, look at Figure 3.1. It shows the monthly performance of the S&P 500 from 1999 through 2008.

As you can see, the stock market fluctuates regularly. No surprise there.

What's interesting, though, is data from the Investment Company Institute. ICI monitors cash flow into and out of stock mutual funds, and its data have clearly shown that, overall, consumers deposit money into stock funds when the stock market is rising, and they withdraw their money when the stock market is falling.

For a closer look at this phenomenon, consider the trading week ending December 5, 2008. That Monday, the Dow Jones Industrial Average dropped 680 points, or 7.7 percent, and investors withdrew $16 billion from their mutual funds.[3] But over the next four days, as the Dow rose 6 percent, investors added $4 billion to their funds.

They sold low and bought high.

They did the exact opposite of what they should be doing.

# Investors Buy When Stocks Are Rising and Sell When Stocks Are Falling

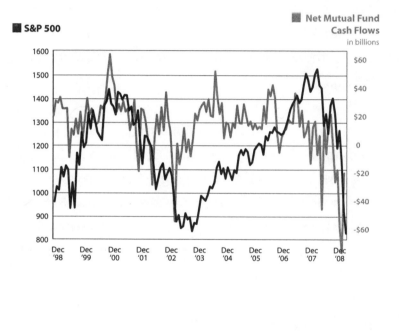

Sources: S&P 500 January 1998–December 2008, Ibbotson Associates. Equity Mutual Fund Net Cash Flows, January 1998–December 2008, Investment Company Institute.

This demonstrates the foolishness of trying to buy low/sell high the way most people try to do it. And believe it or not, I'm actually going to show you how to do it right and how to do it easily.

But to fully understand what I'm about to show you, we need to examine other ways that investors (you?) have tried to achieve success. Again, by studying how others fail, we can better appreciate the correct approach.

### *Following the Fads*

Instead of trying to figure out when to get in or out, some investors try to invest in the latest fad. There's always one or more. In the 1990s it was tech stocks. During the beginning of the twenty-first century, it was real estate. When the economy began to falter in 2008, it seemed like everyone was talking about oil and gold. Now "green" (environmental) stocks are in vogue as we enter the new decade.

What you need to understand is that fads and investing go hand in hand. As long as there have been investments, there have been fads. In fact, the first documented fad was the Dutch Tulip Craze of 1636. At its height, a single tulip bulb sold at auction for today's equivalent of $75,000.[4]

If you think it's impossible for people to pay high prices for worthless items, then you've never heard of Beanie Babies.

The tulip craze wasn't the only time that people paid crazy prices for investments. In 1720 Sir Isaac Newton — generally regarded as a pretty smart guy — was among the many who lost a fortune speculating in the stock of the South Sea Company. Now known as the South Sea Bubble, the speculation ended when the stock's price fell 84 percent.[5]

During the Roaring Twenties, the Dow was up 497 percent at its peak on September 3, 1929. The market then fell 48 percent by November 13, hitting bottom on July 8, 1932, with an 89 percent loss.[6]

Nelson Bunker Hunt and William Herbert Hunt tried to corner the silver market in the 1970s and managed to get the metal to rise 566 percent from 1979 to 1980. The price of silver then fell 77 percent by 1982.[7]

Then there was the Japanese stock market, which rose 3,100 percent between 1965 and 1989. Today, twenty years later, the Nikkei Index is still 65 percent lower than its 1989 high.

Then came Internet mania. From 1994 to 2000, the NASDAQ Stock Market Index jumped 627 percent. After prices peaked on March 10, 2000, the index went on a three-year decline, falling 77 percent by October 9, 2002.[8]

The next fad to emerge was real estate. From 2000 to 2005, the S&P/Case-Shiller Home Price Index grew 102 percent.[9] But like every fad before it, the real estate trend ended swiftly and dramatically, resulting in a deep and prolonged recession.

The real estate debacle didn't satiate investors' hunger for the next fad. For a time, foreign stocks (led by the so-called BRIC nations, Brazil, Russia, India, and China) were all the rage, as were gold and oil, both of which reached all-time highs in 2008 before falling sharply, followed by anything green.

The fascinating aspect of fads is comparing the rises in their prices with the dates investors bought and sold. For example, tech stocks started rising in 1994 — but most of the money that was placed into dot-coms was invested in late 1998 and 1999, well after the bulk of the profits had already been made.[10]

Ditto for the real estate boom. Prices peaked in 2003, but *home sales peaked* in 2005.[11] All the buyers in 2004 and 2005 missed the profits but caught the subsequent losses.

Why is it that people tend to invest in fads *after* the prices have already risen?

# Fads Might Boom,
# But They Always End in Busts

| Event | Boom to Bust | At the Peak | At the Bottom |
|---|---|---|---|
| Tulip Craze[1] | 1634–1636 | +2,000% | −99.9% |
| South Sea Bubble[2] | 1719–1720 | +695% | −84% |
| The Roaring Twenties[3] | 1921–1932 | +497% | −89% |
| Silver Market[4] | 1979–1982 | +566% | −77% |
| Japanese Market[5] | 1965–1992 | +3,100% | −57% |
| Internet Mania[6] | 1994–2002 | +627% | −77% |
| Real Estate Boom[7] | 2000–20?? | +102% | ??% |

[1]Source: UCLA, 2006; [2]Source: Neal, L.D., "How the South Sea Bubble was blown up and burst: A new look at old data," in E.N. White (ed.) *Crashes and Panics*, 1990; [3]Source: stockcharts.com; [4]Source: Bloomberg; [5]Nikkei Stock Index. Source: Ibbotson Associates; [6]NASDAQ. Source: Ibbotson Associates; [7]S&P/Case-Shiller Composite — 20 Metro Home Price Index

The reason is simple: you didn't invest in Internet stocks in 1994 because you hadn't heard about them. It was only in 1998 — after prices had tripled — that tech stocks were featured on the evening news and magazine covers. Likewise, real estate wasn't news in 2000 — but it was in 2004, after people started telling stories about the profits they had earned.

Thus, we buy into fads after the prices have already risen simply because that's when we hear about them. It's another example of buying high/selling low. So if you want to successfully invest in a fad, all you have to do is to buy it before you've ever heard of it.

Ummm, let's try that again.

In other words, people fail to make money in fads because by the time they hear about it, it's too late: the profits have already been obtained.

Investing in fads is simply not a successful investment strategy.

## *Do You Trust the Media?*

The media certainly offer us plenty of investment advice.

Worried about "The Aging Bull Market," the March 11, 1996, cover of *U.S. News & World Report* shouted, "INVESTOR BEWARE!"

I'm not sure what we were supposed to beware, because the Dow gained 17.5 percent from then to the end of the year. The Dow gained another 27 percent in 1997, 25 percent in 1998, and 18 percent in 1999.[12]

In August 1997 *Money* magazine screamed, "Don't Just Sit There . . . SELL STOCK NOW!"

Hope you didn't listen, because the Dow, then at 7694, rose for the rest of that year and the next two.

A year after *Money*'s rant, *Fortune* magazine offered one of its own with a September 28, 1998, cover that predicted "The Crash of '98." Its cover cited "the bouncing Dow" and "a troubled world" as evidence.

Of course, *Fortune* was wrong. There was no crash in 1998. Nor, for that matter, in 1999. Instead, prices kept rising.

Of course, prices did begin to decline in March 2000, and they kept declining for two and a half years. That brings us to October 2, 2002.

On that day, *USA TODAY*'s editors apparently couldn't take it anymore. After all, the Dow had fallen 45 percent since March 2000. So page one of the paper's Money section asked, "Where's the bottom?" with a subhead stating, "No end in sight as day by day Dow sinks away."

With the benefit of hindsight, we now know when the bottom occurred. It was October 2, 2002 — the very day *USA TODAY* asked the question.

What about CNBC's Jim Cramer, who offers a barrage of advice on each night's broadcast? *Barron's* studied each of Cramer's recommendations in 2006 and 2007, and in its August 20, 2007, issue concluded that his picks gained an average of 12 percent.

*Barron's* noted that for the same period the S&P 500 gained 22 percent. Cramer was about half as good.

Cramer's mania can sometimes be astonishing to witness. On Friday, June 27, 2008, a day after the Dow fell 358 points, he wrote in his daily online column, "Sell everything. Nothing's working. Revisit when the prices are adjusted for a big recession, soaring inflation and a crushed consumer. Sell at 12,000 and come back at 10,000. Even better: Short it."

Then, just two business days later (Tuesday, July 1), in a column titled "10 Reasons the Rally Could Last," he wrote: "This is a real turnaround from hopelessness, while it will be hard for the bears to believe that they might actually be on the receiving end of the pain. I have to believe that it can last for more than one day."

What had happened between Cramer's Friday panic (sell everything!) and Tuesday's euphoria (this is a real turnaround!)?

Apparently, nothing: on Monday the Dow had gained three points.

Then there's the case of *Forbes* columnist Lisa Hess. In the March 10, 2008, issue, she recommended that readers invest in Fannie Mae.

At the time, the stock was selling for about $35 a share.

Looking back, we now know that her advice was pretty bad.

By September 1, the stock had fallen to $6.84.

So, in her September 15 column, Lisa apologized for her March recommendation — and told readers to sell Fannie Mae . . . *and buy Freddie Mac!*

By the time the issue reached newsstands, the government had taken over both Fannie and Freddie, and the stocks were virtually worthless.

*Fortune* magazine offered similarly bad advice in its *2007 Investor Guide.* Published in December 2006, the guide featured "The 10 Stocks to Buy Now." American International Group was one of its picks. As we know, AIG was taken over by the federal government, and its stock price fell 98 percent in the next 21 months.

So, in its next annual guide, *Fortune* apologized and made amends by offering a new pick: Merrill Lynch, which was acquired by Bank of America after Merrill Lynch's stock fell 78 percent in 2008.

All told, *Fortune*'s ten stock picks for 2008 fell an average of 47 percent, while the S&P 500 fell 38.5 percent.[13]

But my favorite example of all comes from *Money* magazine. In March 1994 the publication's cover touted "Eight Top Investments That Never Lose Money."

By the end of the year, seven of them did.

The examples are endless; an academic study showed that investors who follow media recommendations lose, on average, 3.8 percent of their money in the following six months.[14]

Clearly, trusting the media's investment advice is not a successful strategy. Yet judging from the millions of people who read, listen, and watch all the commentaries, it's also clear that most people don't know this.

### *Not-So-Expert Advice*

If we can't trust the media to help us make good investments, we should at least be able to consult the experts, right?

The problem is that the experts never agree.

At any given moment, on any given issue, you can find many experts predicting one result and just as many predicting another. With so many thousands of economists, market analysts, portfolio managers, and traders, in fact, each year is certain to find *someone* who correctly predicted the topic *du jour*.

Problem is, it's almost never the same person twice.

There aren't many people who would invest their life savings on the prognostications of a TV weatherman or a sportswriter — we all know their predictions prove to be notoriously inaccurate — yet millions invest their money based on the musings of a single money manager.

Consider the case of Jason Trennert, *USA Today*'s "top strategist for 2008." He predicted that stock prices would rise 14 percent in 2008. Instead the S&P 500 fell 38.5 percent. (As bumbling TV spy Maxwell Smart would say, "missed it by *that* much.")

With all the golf swings made every year, *someone* is going to hit the ball into that little hole for a hole in one. With all the baseball games played every year, *someone* is going to pitch a no-hitter. Sports fans know that the hole in one won't necessarily be hit by the best player, nor will the perfect game be pitched by the best pitcher. But *someone* will do it.

Sometimes people get it right. Sometimes they get it wrong.

It doesn't surprise us when the weathermen get it wrong. It doesn't surprise us when sportswriters get it wrong. Why, then, does it surprise us to think that an investment analyst or portfolio manager might be wrong? And why are so many people willing to invest their life savings on the prognostications of such a person?

Predictions are not reliable in sports, nor about the weather, nor on Wall Street.

Don't rely on experts.

## *Don't Count On Quality*

Many investors, daunted by the challenge of picking the right investments, simply default to the oldest, biggest, best-known, and most popular companies in America. How could you go wrong with that?

Take a company like DuPont. Founded in 1802, it is one of the best-known in the world. The company operates in 70 countries, has 60,000 employees, spends $1 billion annually on research and development in 75 labs in 12 countries, and had 2008 revenues of $31 billion. Its many products include cellophane, Freon, nylon, Teflon, Dacron, Lycra, Kevlar, and Corian.[15]

From 1990 to 1998, its stock tripled in value.

But if you owned its stock during the nine years from 1998 to 2006, your shares would have lost 29 percent of their value.

FIGURE 3.3

# Are the Best Known Companies Really the Best Investments?

| Company | Stock Performance | Period |
|---|---|---|
| DuPont | 29% loss in 9 years | 1998–2006 |
| Disney | 51% loss in 5 years | 1998–2002 |
| GE | 53% loss in 3 years | 2000–2002 |
| GM | 95% loss in 8 years | 2000–2008 |
| Honeywell | 58% loss in 3 years | 2000–2002 |
| Hewlett-Packard | 61% loss in 3 years | 2000–2002 |
| IBM | 36% loss in 1 year | 2002 |
| JPMorgan Chase & Co. | 54% loss in 3 years | 2000–2002 |
| Coca-Cola | 40% loss in 7 years | 1999–2005 |
| Coca-Cola | 26% loss in 1 year | 2008 |
| McDonald's | 60% loss in 3 years | 2000–2002 |
| Altria | 57% loss in 1 year | 1999 |
| Merck | 66% loss in 4 years | 2001–2004 |
| Procter & Gamble | 28% loss in 1 year | 2000 |
| AT&T | 54% loss in 7 years | 1999–2005 |
| Wal-Mart | 37% loss in 8 years | 2000–2007 |
| Exxon | 20% loss in 2 years | 2001–2002 |
| Merrill Lynch | 78% loss in 1 year | 2008 |
| AIG | 97% loss in 1 year | 2008 |
| Fannie Mae | 98% loss in 1 year | 2008 |
| Freddie Mac | 98% loss in 1 year | 2008 |
| Wachovia | 85% loss in 1 year | 2008 |
| MBIA | 78% loss in 1 year | 2008 |
| AMBAC | 95% loss in 1 year | 2008 |
| S&P 500 | 49% have lower prices than in 2000 | |

Source: Bloomberg as of December 31, 2008

Or you could have invested in the Walt Disney Company. As Figure 3.3 shows, its stock fell 51 percent over five years.

McDonald's stock lost 60 percent over three years.

General Electric's stock price dropped 13 percent *in a single day* (April 11, 2008).

It's the same story at Honeywell International, Hewlett-Packard, IBM, JPMorgan Chase & Co., and dozens of other big-name companies. In fact, 49 percent of the stocks in the S&P 500 were lower in 2008 than they were in 2000.[16]

Clearly, investing in a large, well-established company does not mean that you are immune from suffering massive losses over extended periods of time. Yet millions of Americans entrust these companies with their future financial security.

As a financial advisor who has counseled thousands of people during my career, I have seen people make this error many times. They invest their life savings into a single stock: that of their employer. Others invest most of their money into a single company because they like its product. This mistake is so common that I've given it a name: *Enron-itis.*

In 2001, Enron was the seventh-largest company in America, according to the Fortune 500.

That was the year it went broke.

It was also the year of my first television appearance on *The Oprah Winfrey Show*. Oprah asked me to counsel a woman caught up in Enron's collapse. A former mid-level employee of the company, she had more than $2 million in Enron stock in her 401(k) account. When the company went broke, she lost both her job and the $2 million.

Today millions of workers still persist in this same behavior.

A 2008 survey of 1.8 million employees of three hundred companies by Hewitt Associates found that nearly 22 percent of the assets in 401(k) plans consist of the employer's stock — the most commonly owned investment in those plans.

At some companies, it's even worse.

For instance, Sherwin-Williams workers have placed 92 percent of their 401(k) assets in company stock. Employees at Pfizer have 86 percent of their 401(k) assets in company stock, and the figure is 74 percent at McDonald's.[17] Those are just three examples. There are hundreds of others.

Do you really want to risk your financial security on the fortunes of a company over which you have little knowledge and no control? Clearly, that's a foolish bet.

You cannot count on quality for your financial security.

## Hot Sectors That Aren't

Some investors recognize the foolishness of investing in specific stocks.

After all, even though the airline industry will survive, that doesn't mean certain airlines will.

Therefore, some investors conclude, it's better to select a broad-based sector of the stock market instead of a single company or even a single industry. They figure it's better to split stocks into two categories, such as growth stocks and value stocks.

Or large companies and small companies.

Or U.S. stocks and foreign stocks.

Then, they figure, you just invest in the one group that will do better than the other.

But how do you do that?

It's a question that many investors try to answer.

It's impossible.

The performance of all these groups from 1989 through 2008 is shown in Figures 3.4 to 3.6.

As you can see, in any given year, one beats the other.

But it's impossible to predict which one will do better the following year.

And yet, many investors insist on trying.

FIGURE 3.4

# Growth Stocks vs. Value Stocks
## 1984–2008

## One Beats the Other Each Year

| 1984 | Value | 1997 | Value |
|------|--------|------|--------|
| 1985 | Growth | 1998 | Growth |
| 1986 | Value | 1999 | Growth |
| 1987 | Growth | 2000 | Value |
| 1988 | Value | 2001 | Value |
| 1989 | Growth | 2002 | Value |
| 1990 | Growth | 2003 | Value |
| 1991 | Growth | 2004 | Value |
| 1992 | Value | 2005 | Value |
| 1993 | Value | 2006 | Value |
| 1994 | Growth | 2007 | Growth |
| 1995 | Value | 2008 | Value |
| 1996 | Growth | 2009 | ??? |

## Can You Predict Which Will Perform Best in 2009?

Russell 3000 Growth Index and Russell 3000 Value Index. Source: Ibbotson Associates. Past performance does not guarantee future results.

FIGURE 3.5

# Large Stocks vs. Small Stocks
## 1984–2008

## One Beats the Other Each Year

| | | | |
|---|---|---|---|
| 1984 | Large | 1997 | Large |
| 1985 | Large | 1998 | Large |
| 1986 | Large | 1999 | Small |
| 1987 | Large | 2000 | Small |
| 1988 | Small | 2001 | Small |
| 1989 | Large | 2002 | Small |
| 1990 | Large | 2003 | Small |
| 1991 | Small | 2004 | Small |
| 1992 | Small | 2005 | Large |
| 1993 | Small | 2006 | Small |
| 1994 | Large | 2007 | Large |
| 1995 | Large | 2008 | Small |
| 1996 | Large | 2009 | ??? |

## Can You Predict Which
## Will Perform Best in 2009?

Russell 1000 Stock Index and Russell 2000 Stock Index. Source: Ibbotson Associates. Past performance does not guarantee future results.

# FIGURE 3.6

## U.S. Stocks vs. Foreign Stocks
## 1984–2008

### One Beats the Other Each Year

| Year | Winner | Year | Winner |
|------|--------|------|--------|
| 1984 | Foreign | 1997 | U.S. |
| 1985 | Foreign | 1998 | U.S. |
| 1986 | Foreign | 1999 | Foreign |
| 1987 | Foreign | 2000 | U.S. |
| 1988 | Foreign | 2001 | U.S. |
| 1989 | U.S. | 2002 | Foreign |
| 1990 | U.S. | 2003 | Foreign |
| 1991 | U.S. | 2004 | Foreign |
| 1992 | U.S. | 2005 | Foreign |
| 1993 | Foreign | 2006 | Foreign |
| 1994 | Foreign | 2007 | Foreign |
| 1995 | U.S. | 2008 | U.S. |
| 1996 | U.S. | 2009 | ??? |

### Can You Predict Which
### Will Perform Best in 2009?

MSCI EAFE Index and Russell 3000 Stock Index. Source: Ibbotson Associates. Past performance does not guarantee future results.

# *The Two "Truths" That Prevent You from Investing Successfully*

So far we've learned that market timing doesn't work. Nor should you follow fads, trust the media, rely on so-called experts, or make big bets on blue-chip stocks or hot sectors.

None of these ideas works, yet many investors persist in relying on these strategies. When one fails, they simply move to the next, confidently believing (or merely hoping) that it will pay off.

Why do investors do this? Because they believe in two basic truths:

> 1. Stock prices rise and fall.
>
> 2. The stock market is risky, volatile, and unpredictable.

Do you agree with these statements?

Let's explore them.

### *Basic Truth 1: Stock Prices Rise and Fall*

Of course, literally speaking, this statement is true. But it's misleading. That's because the statement is incomplete; it's not really accurate to say that stock prices "rise and fall."

Oh, sure, on any given day, prices might rise or fall. But over long periods, it's more accurate to say that prices in the overall stock market rise *a lot* but fall *a little,* as shown by Figure 4.1.

FIGURE 4.1

# Bull and Bear Markets
## The S&P 500 from 1949–2008

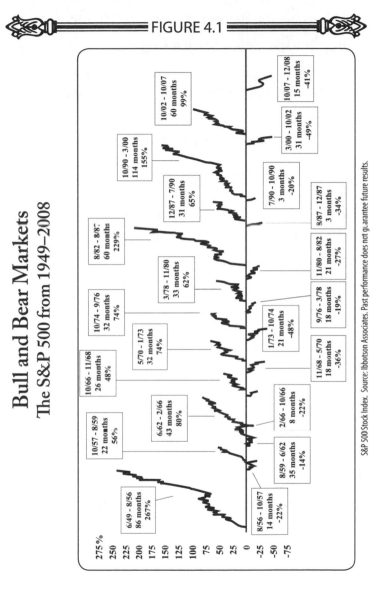

| | |
|---|---|
| 6/49 - 8/56<br>86 months<br>267% | |
| 8/56 - 10/57<br>14 months<br>-22% | |
| 10/57 - 8/59<br>22 months<br>56% | |
| 8/59 - 6/62<br>35 months<br>-14% | |
| 6/62 - 2/66<br>43 months<br>80% | |
| 2/66 - 10/66<br>8 months<br>-22% | |
| 10/66 - 11/68<br>26 months<br>48% | |
| 11/68 - 5/70<br>18 months<br>-36% | |
| 5/70 - 1/73<br>32 months<br>74% | |
| 1/73 - 10/74<br>21 months<br>-48% | |
| 10/74 - 9/76<br>32 months<br>74% | |
| 9/76 - 3/78<br>18 months<br>-19% | |
| 3/78 - 11/80<br>33 months<br>62% | |
| 11/80 - 8/82<br>21 months<br>-27% | |
| 8/82 - 8/87<br>60 months<br>229% | |
| 8/87 - 12/87<br>3 months<br>-34% | |
| 12/87 - 7/90<br>31 months<br>65% | |
| 7/90 - 10/90<br>3 months<br>-20% | |
| 10/90 - 3/00<br>114 months<br>155% | |
| 3/00 - 10/02<br>31 months<br>-49% | |
| 10/02 - 10/07<br>60 months<br>99% | |
| 10/07 - 12/08<br>15 months<br>-41% | |

S&P 500 Stock Index.   Source: Ibbotson Associates.   Past performance does not guarantee future results.

This chart clearly shows that when stock prices are rising, they rise *a lot* and for a *long time*.

When prices fall, they fall *a little* and for a *short period*.

This explains the real reason why the stock market is able to exist.

Think about it. If stock prices were to only rise and fall, there would never be growth in the economy. It would force investors to decide when to buy and when to sell.

Imagine playing with a yo-yo. It goes down, then it comes up. Down, up. Down, up. If that yo-yo were a stock's price, the trick would be to catch it and release it at the right time. But as the chart shows, investing in the stock market is like playing with a yo-yo while climbing a hill. Even though the yo-yo is still going down, up, down, up, the height of the yo-yo is constantly climbing, thanks to the hill's incline.

Here's another way to put it: The market doesn't simply go up one point and then down one point. Rather, it goes up two points, then down one point. Then it goes up four, down one, up three and down one. Sure, sometimes the down is larger than the previous up, but over long periods, the stock market has always produced net profits. That's why it's wrong to be upset when stock prices fall. Instead of lamenting the current decline, focus on what is about to happen next. This point is particularly important following 2008's terrible performance.

But if you had the opportunity to invest at the moment of your choosing, where on Figure 4.1 would you choose? And where are we on that chart right now?

When you notice that stock prices are declining, don't be upset. Instead become excited about what lies ahead.

## *Basic Truth 2: The Stock Market Is Risky, Volatile, and Unpredictable*

If you believe this truth, that's because you're familiar with the chart in Figure 4.2. It shows the monthly performance of the S&P 500 since 1926.

Clearly, the stock market is volatile. It's also unpredictable. No one can say what will happen next by looking at that chart. And that makes the stock market risky. It's like driving a car blindfolded.

But does this chart really matter?

Think about the last time you invested money; whether you bought a stock, a bond, a mutual fund, some real estate, or added to your retirement account at work — whatever. Now let me ask you a question: When you invested that money, was it your intention to withdraw the money in just thirty days?

FIGURE 4.2

# Monthly Performance of the S&P 500 1926–2008

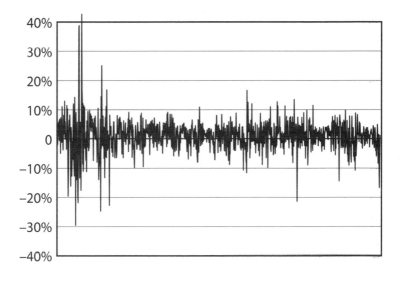

Monthly performance of the S&P 500 Stock Index 1926–2008. Source: Ibbotson Associates.
Past performance does not guarantee future results.

Of course not. Your plan, more likely, was to leave the money alone for years, maybe even decades. So why, then, does the chart in Figure 4.2 matter?

Yet that's how investors — spurred by the media — view the market. They watch it day by day and (in the case of CNBC) moment by moment.

But how could today's movements matter if you're investing for your child's college education or your own retirement?

So let's stretch our view of the stock market. Instead of a month-by-month review, let's see how it performs over fifteen-year periods, as shown in Figure 4.3.

As you can see, when viewed over long periods of time, the stock market isn't nearly so unpredictable. It's not so volatile either, and that means it's not nearly as risky as you thought.

This is why the best way to view the stock market is over decades, not days, weeks, or months.

# FIGURE 4.3

# Fifteen-Year Performance
# of the S&P 500
# 1926–2008

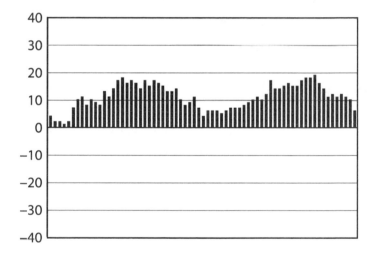

Fifteen-year rolling intervals of the S&P 500 Stock Index 1926–2008. Source: Ibbotson Associates.
Past performance does not guarantee future results.

But investors don't understand this. That's why they rip open the envelope as soon as their monthly account statement arrives. Many peruse the pricing tables in the newspaper every day. Some check the prices on the Internet throughout the day.

But if you're seeking to achieve a long-term goal such as college or retirement, why bother looking at your account each hour, day, or month? Stop looking. Find something else to do.

### *Why You Mustn't Look*

Looking often at your investments is likely to make you do the opposite of what you should do. If you see that prices are down, you'll become upset and want to sell. If you see that prices are up, you'll get excited and want to buy.

You'll be tempted to sell low and buy high.

Sound familiar?

This is why you must stop watching the news. The media report only what's happening today, making you think that today matters. I've never heard a news anchor say, "As of today, the stock market's average annual return for the past twenty years is 8.4 percent." Yet that information would be more useful to investors than reporting today's results.

## The Truth About the Two Basic Truths

Now you know the truth: the two basic truths are really nothing more than common myths. And by mistaking these myths as truths, Americans set themselves up for investment failure.

Relying on these myths causes people to engage in strategies that don't work, such as trying to buy low/sell high. Following fads. Listening to the media. Relying on experts. Counting on quality. Picking hot sectors.

Dismiss these concoctions and instead believe that the stock market produces profits over long periods. You believe this, after all. Let me prove it to you.

# Answer this question:

Twenty years from now, do you believe that the Dow will be higher than it is today?

I often ask this question in my seminars. Never has anyone said that the stock market will be lower in twenty years than it is at the moment. So I'll assume that you also agree that the market will be higher in the future.

One more question, if you please.

Take a guess at what the stock market's average annual rate of return will be over the next twenty years. This question is a bit harder to answer, so look at Figure 4.4 for some statistics that might help.

# So I'll ask again:

What do you guess will be the market's average annual rate of return over the next twenty years?

FIGURE 4.4

**1926–2008** { *The average return was 9.6% per year.*

**1989–2008** { *The average return was 8.4% per year.*

**1990-1999** { *The average return was 18.2% per year.*

**2000–2008** { *The average return was –3.6% per year.*

Data reflect performance of the S&P 500 Stock Index. Source: Ibbotson Associates.
Past performance does not guarantee future results.

As of January 1, 2009, the Dow Jones Industrial Average was 8776.

If the Dow grows 12 percent annually over the next twenty years, it will be 84,656 in 2029.

If the Dow grows 10 percent annually over the next twenty years, it will be 59,041 in 2029.

If the Dow grows 7 percent annually over the next twenty years, it will be 33,960 in 2029.

If the Dow grows 3.5 percent annually over the next twenty years, it will be 17,426 in 2029.

The *worst* twenty-year performance for the stock market since 1926 is 3.1 percent, which would put the Dow at 16,161 in 2029.[18]

The *average* twenty-year performance since 1926 is 11.4 percent, which would put the Dow at 76,033.[19]

So instead of being afraid of investments, maybe you ought to get excited.

## A Cautionary Tale

But let's not get *too* excited.

Even though it is reasonable to expect the stock market to grow over the next twenty years, we need to put this discovery into proper context.

Yes, the stock market can be expected to perform quite nicely over very long periods. Even at a very low annual rate of return, the Dow will double in twenty years.

So allow me to share a story with you.

It's a true story, but I hasten to add that the individual involved was not my client. (I met this gentleman after the following story occurred. In fact, that's why I met him; he came to my firm for help.)

His story begins in 1990. He was fifty years old and had $250,000 in his retirement plan at work, invested entirely in stock mutual funds.

He planned to retire at age sixty-five.

On January 1, 1990, the Dow was 2753. Ten years later, on December 31, 1999, the Dow was 11,497. Amazingly, it had more than quadrupled in value.

Like all other Investors, this gentleman saw his mutual funds skyrocket in value. His retirement account had quadrupled, growing to $1 million.

He never expected to accumulate so much money, and certainly not by age sixty.

So, having met his retirement goal, he decided to retire and live the life of comfort that he'd long planned — and he got to begin five years earlier than he had expected.

He also decided to leave his money invested in the same funds that he'd owned the past ten years, since he was so pleased with their performance. After all, they had quadrupled in value in just ten years. Imagine what they would do over the next ten!

He didn't have to imagine. He *knew* they would quadruple again. In another ten years, the Dow would be at 45,988, and at age seventy he would be worth $4 million.

Well, that was 1999. We know what happened over the next three years.

From 2000 to 2002, the stock market didn't continue to rise. Instead stocks fell 45 percent.

The gentleman didn't discover that his account was worth 45 percent less after three years, however. You see, because he was retired and not yet eligible for Social Security or a pension, he had been withdrawing money from his account.

Thus, between his withdrawals and a declining market, by the end of 2002 his account had fallen to the same value it had been in 1990: $250,000.

And so, at age sixty-three, he had to go back to work.

This is why, no matter how excited, optimistic, or confident we might be about how the stock market will perform over long periods, we must be careful.

After all, the stock market could crash the day you retire.

(And I know you're thinking that, with your luck, it probably will!)

FIGURE 4.5

# A Sad Story
## Don't let this happen to you

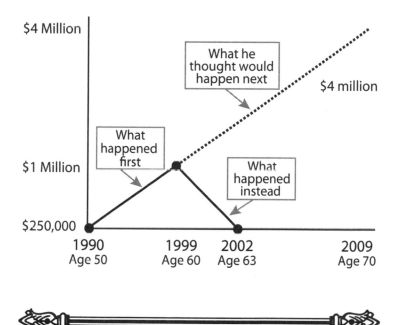

$4 Million

What he
thought would
happen next

$4 million

What
happened
first

$1 Million

What
happened
instead

$250,000

1990
Age 50

1999
Age 60

2002
Age 63

2009
Age 70

Illustrative story is anecdotal and not indicative of any specific investment.
Past performance does not guarantee future results.

# *The Secret*

Stocks might crash.

Bonds can fall.

Real estate may collapse.

Gold and oil prices can plummet.

Banks can fail.

Money market funds can "break the buck" (lose money and prohibit withdrawals).

Interest rates can approach zero, meaning that it can cost more to buy U.S. Treasuries than you earn in interest.

So what's an investor to do?

The answer is simple: do everything.

As investors learned painfully in the 2000s, there are times, however unusual, when there is no safe place to hide. Even in more normal times (which means pretty much any moment other than the 2000s), there's always one investment that's doing poorly while others are doing well.

It's easy to talk about what has done well, but no one is able to predict with any consistency what is *about* to do well.

Therefore, you must buy everything. Do it all. In other words, diversify.

When I began my career as a financial advisor in the mid-1980s, diversification was an unknown concept for most consumers. By now, you've probably heard about it. But I suspect that you don't fully understand it and thus don't know how to effectively execute it. So let me explain it to you.

Figure 5.1 shows how each of sixteen asset classes and market sectors performed each year from 1999 through 2008.

Examine each column, and you'll see that there is no pattern. It is impossible to predict, based on each asset class or market sector's past performance, whether one will perform better or worse than the others in the following year.

Now let me show you how to use this chart to your advantage.

FIGURE 5.1

## Asset Class Performance 1999–2008
### Ranked 1 (best) – 16 (worst)

| | Commodities | Emerging Markets | Oil & Gas | Gold | Foreign Stocks | SmallCap Growth | MidCap Growth | LargeCap Growth |
|---|---|---|---|---|---|---|---|---|
| **1999** | 6 | 1 | 7 | 12 | 5 | 4 | 2 | 3 |
| **2000** | 1 | 16 | 3 | 10 | 13 | 15 | 12 | 14 |
| **2001** | 13 | 9 | 11 | 7 | 16 | 14 | 15 | 12 |
| **2002** | 1 | 8 | 10 | 2 | 12 | 15 | 14 | 16 |
| **2003** | 12 | 1 | 11 | 13 | 3 | 7 | 2 | 10 |
| **2004** | 10 | 4 | 1 | 14 | 5 | 13 | 7 | 12 |
| **2005** | 3 | 2 | 1 | 4 | 5 | 12 | 7 | 16 |
| **2006** | 15 | 2 | 5 | 4 | 3 | 12 | 11 | 10 |
| **2007** | 4 | 1 | 2 | 3 | 5 | 7 | 6 | 9 |
| **2008** | 7 | 16 | 8 | 4 | 14 | 10 | 15 | 6 |

Data reflect the Russell 3000 Growth TR, Russell Mid Cap Growth TR, S&P 500/Citi Growth TR, BarCap US Treasury Long TR, BarCap Interm US Treasury TR, IA SBBI US 1 Yr Trsy Const Matl TR, Russell 3000 Value TR, Russell Mid Cap Value TR, S&P 500/Citi Value TR, BarCap US Corporate High Yield TR, DJ US Real Estate TR for the ten-year period ending December 31, 2008. Past performance does not guarantee future results.

FIGURE 5.1

# Asset Class Performance 1999–2008

## Ranked 1 (best) – 16 (worst)

| | Long-Term Bonds | Intermediate Term Bonds | Short-Term Bonds | SmallCap Value | MidCap Value | LargeCap Value | Junk Bonds | Real Estate |
|---|---|---|---|---|---|---|---|---|
| **1999** | 16 | 13 | 10 | 8 | 14 | 9 | 11 | 15 |
| **2000** | 4 | 6 | 8 | 7 | 5 | 9 | 11 | 2 |
| **2001** | 5 | 2 | 3 | 8 | 6 | 10 | 4 | 1 |
| **2002** | 3 | 4 | 6 | 11 | 9 | 13 | 7 | 5 |
| **2003** | 14 | 15 | 16 | 6 | 4 | 8 | 9 | 5 |
| **2004** | 11 | 15 | 16 | 6 | 3 | 8 | 9 | 2 |
| **2005** | 11 | 15 | 14 | 10 | 6 | 9 | 13 | 8 |
| **2006** | 16 | 14 | 13 | 6 | 8 | 7 | 9 | 1 |
| **2007** | 8 | 10 | 11 | 14 | 15 | 12 | 13 | 16 |
| **2008** | 1 | 2 | 3 | 9 | 11 | 12 | 5 | 13 |

Data reflect the Russell 3000 Growth TR, Russell Mid Cap Growth TR, S&P 500/Citi Growth TR, BarCap US Treasury Long TR, BarCap Interm US Treasury TR, IA SBBI US 1 Yr Trsy Const Matl TR, Russell 3000 Value TR, Russell Mid Cap Value TR, S&P 500/ Citi Value TR, BarCap US Corporate High Yield TR, DJ US Real Estate TR for the ten-year period ending December 31, 2008. Past performance does not guarantee future results.

If you invested the same amount into all sixteen of those major asset classes and market sectors during that ten-year period, you would have earned an average of 5 percent per year. But if you failed to invest in the two best-performing asset classes of each year, your average return would have been only 1.8 percent.[20]

Now, I am an expert in personal finance. My firm manages billions of dollars, and we've been managing money for more than two decades. And yet I readily admit that my colleagues and I can't predict with any certainty which asset class or market sectors will do best next year.

I am willing to admit that we don't know. Are you willing to admit that you don't know either?

After all, there are only two kinds of investors: those who don't know, and those who don't know that they don't know.

FIGURE 5.2

# Investing in Fourteen vs. Sixteen of the Markets 1999–2008

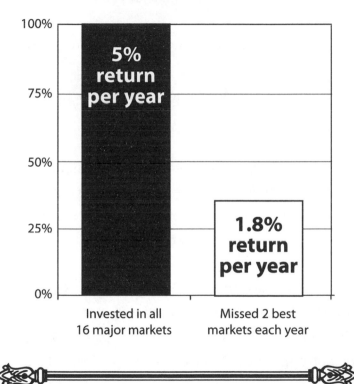

| | |
|---|---|
| 5% return per year | 1.8% return per year |
| Invested in all 16 major markets | Missed 2 best markets each year |

Source: Ibbotson Associates. Data reflect the Russell 3000 Growth TR, Russell Mid Cap Growth TR, S&P 500/Citi Growth TR, BarCap US Treasury Long TR, BarCap Interm US Treasury TR, IA SBBI US 1 Yr Trsy Const Matl TR, Russell 3000 Value TR, Russell Mid Cap Value TR, S&P 500/Citi Value TR, BarCap US Corporate High Yield TR, DJ US Real Estate TR for the ten-year period ending December 31, 2008. Past performance does not guarantee future results.

## *It's a Game of Horseshoes, Not a Horse Race*

Now you understand the trick that's being played on you by the personal finance media. They try to trick you into thinking that investing is like a horse race: you'd better pick the right horse or you'll be broke.

But you don't know how to pick the right investments.

You know that you don't know how to pick the right investments.

The so-called experts in the media know that you know that you don't know how to pick the right investments. They don't know how to pick them either. But they pretend that they do.

Hence, headlines such as *U.S. News & World Report*'s "Investor Beware!" in 1996, *Money*'s "Sell Stock Now" in 1996, *Fortune*'s "The Crash of '98," *USA Today*'s "Where's the bottom?" in 2002, *Fortune*'s "The 10 Stocks to Buy Now" in 2006 and 2007, and *Money*'s "Eight Top Investments That Never Lose Money."

Since you know that you don't know how to pick the right investments, and since the experts act like they do know how (are you following all this?), you follow their advice.

I have news for you. Investing is not a horse race. You don't have to pick the winner. Instead, investing is a game of horseshoes. Being close is good enough to win. Warren Buffett said it best: "It is better to be approximately right than precisely wrong."

## *Something Else the Media Never Tell You*

All those media predictions have two points in common.

First, as you well know, the finance media brag about how much money their tips will make you. But there's another element common to financial writers, one that you might not have realized.

They fail to tell you how much risk you're taking by acting on their tips.

Think about it: when Jim Cramer or *Money* magazine touts a hot stock, there's nary a mention of the risk you'll be taking to get those returns. You know that investing is as much about risk as it is about return. Yet the media highlight the latter and ignore the former. This is an amazing omission because you are very interested in risk, and correctly so.

If you're not sure that you're concerned about risk, consider this illustration: traveling by car from Washington, D.C., to New York City typically takes about four hours. If I sped to get you there in just ninety minutes, would you reward me for my performance or chastise me for the risk I forced you to take? Methinks you'd chastise me.

All investors must resolve these competing goals. You desire high returns. You want to avoid big losses.

To show you how diversification can help, let's examine the performance of four different portfolios during the period of 1972 through 1992. I chose this twenty-year period because it covers the recessionary seventies as well as the bull market of the eighties.

The stock market is as risky as it gets. Figure 5.3 shows the volatility of a portfolio that's invested entirely in stocks. (Our volatility measurement is based on standard deviation, which is explained in both *The Truth About Money* and *Discover the Wealth Within You*.)

Compared to that portfolio are three others. One invests 100 percent in bonds; another invests equally in stocks, bonds, and cash; and the third invests equally in stocks, bonds, cash, foreign stocks, and real estate. As Figure 5.3 shows, the portfolio that had the greatest level of diversification enjoyed the lowest amount of risk.

That's no surprise. After all, that's the main reason people like to diversify: to lower their risk. But some people hesitate because they are familiar with that risk-reward equation. If they lower their risk, they fear that they also lower their return.

FIGURE 5.3

# Volatility
## 1972–1992

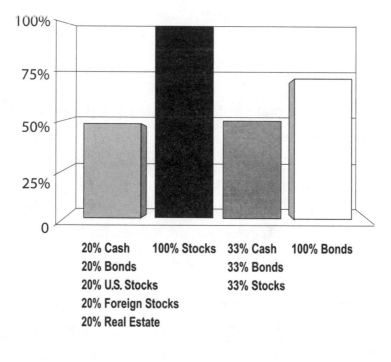

Measure of Standard Deviation. Source: Ibbotson Associates. Past performance is not a guarantee of future results.

But it doesn't have to be so. Take a look at Figure 5.4, which reveals the returns generated by each of those four portfolios over that same time period. As you can see, that highly diversified portfolio generated average returns that were as good as those produced by the portfolio that owned nothing but stocks.

In other words, lowering the risk does not necessarily mean that you lower the returns. It's possible to enjoy the returns you want while avoiding the risks you don't want.

### *Optimizing Versus Maximizing*

To understand this concept, let me offer you two investment choices.

One investment earns 10 percent.

The other earns 8 percent but has only half the risk.

Which one do you prefer?

FIGURE 5.4

# Average Annual Returns
## 1972–1992

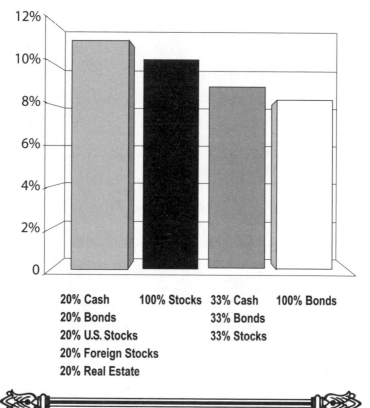

| | | | |
|---|---|---|---|
| 20% Cash | 100% Stocks | 33% Cash | 100% Bonds |
| 20% Bonds | | 33% Bonds | |
| 20% U.S. Stocks | | 33% Stocks | |
| 20% Foreign Stocks | | | |
| 20% Real Estate | | | |

Source: Ibbotson Associates. Past performance is not a guarantee of future results.

When I pose this question at my seminars, almost everyone prefers the 8 percent investment. A few, however, say that they would rather earn 10 percent than 8 percent and are willing to expose themselves to the volatility that seeking such returns requires.

This evaluation is what Wall Street calls *portfolio optimization* versus *portfolio maximization*.

The maximizer doesn't care (or professes not to care) about risk. He loves roller coasters.

The optimizer cares very much about risk. He doesn't want to throw up.

I've learned through decades of working with individuals just like you that most of the people who had claimed to be maximizers felt that way only before they experienced the very risks they had claimed not to mind.

This became particularly apparent in 2008. Many people had no idea that they could lose 60 percent or 70 percent of their life savings in a matter of months. Now, unfortunately, they've learned, somewhat too late, that they don't have the stomach for it.

A merry-go-round is a much smoother ride, and it ends up at the same place as the roller coaster. Without making you nauseous.

*If you don't know
who you are, the
stock market is a very
expensive place to
find out.*

— *George Goodman*

# *The Secret to the Secret*

Diversification is a proven approach to investment success. Of course, no strategy can guarantee profits or eliminate the risk of investment losses.

But to succeed with this approach, you must apply two crucial elements. Let's explore them.

### *Crucial Step 1: Maintain a Long-term Focus*

You must maintain a long-term focus for one simple reason: it's the only way that you can be certain that you'll capture the profits that investments offer.

To illustrate, let's look at Figure 6.1. It displays the S&P 500 in 2007, a year when it gained 5.5 percent. Considering that the stock market has averaged 9.6 percent per year from 1926 to 2008,[21] a 5.5 percent gain isn't great.

And 2007 is even worse than you think. That's because from January 1 to November 21 of that year, the stock market gained nothing. Indeed, the S&P 500 stood at 1418 on January 1, and it was virtually the same — 1417 — on November 21.

Then, from November 21 to November 28, the stock market jumped 5.5 percent. After that, the market remained flat for the rest of the year.

We didn't have a good year in 2007; we had a good week!

# FIGURE 6.1

# S&P 500
## 2007
## The Entire Gain Occurred in Just 1 Week

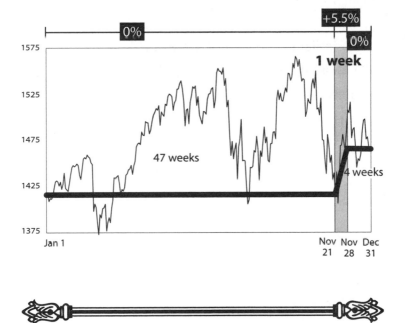

Performance of the S&P 500 Stock Index from Jan. 1, 2007 through Dec. 31, 2007. Source: Ibbotson Associates.
Past performance does not guarantee future results.

Amazingly, 2007 was not unusual. We had a similar experience in 2006. As Figure 6.2 shows, the stock market's entire profit of 13.6 percent occurred in only eighteen weeks.

In 2005, the year's profit occurred in eight weeks.

In 2004, seven weeks.

It was similar in 2003, 1999, 1998, 1997, 1996, 1992, 1991 — all shown by Figures 6.3 through 6.11. You get the point.

FIGURE 6.2

# S&P 500
## 2006
### The Entire Gain Occurred in Just 18 Weeks

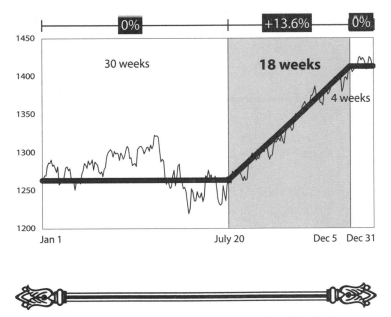

Performance of the S&P 500 Index from Jan. 1, 2006 through Dec. 31, 2006. Source: Ibbotson Associates.
Past performance does not guarantee future results.

# S&P 500
## 2005
### The Entire Gain Occurred in Just 8 Weeks

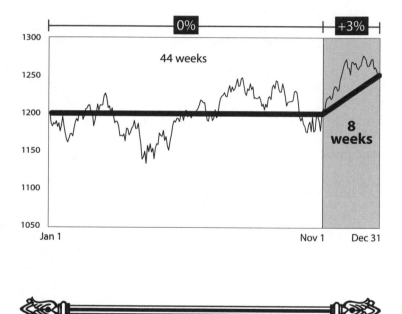

Performance of the S&P 500 Index from Jan. 1, 2005 through Dec. 31, 2005. Source: Ibbotson Associates.
Past performance does not guarantee future results.

# FIGURE 6.4

# S&P 500
## 2004
### The Entire Gain Occurred in Just 7 Weeks

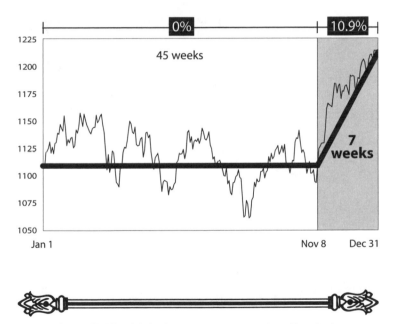

Performance of the S&P 500 Index from Jan. 1, 2004 through Dec. 31, 2004. Source: Ibbotson Associates.
Past performance does not guarantee future results.

# FIGURE 6.5

# S&P 500
## 2003
## The Entire Gain Occurred in Just 16 Weeks

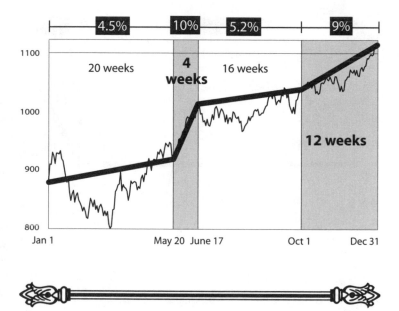

Performance of the S&P 500 Index from Jan. 1, 2003 through Dec. 31, 2003. Source: Ibbotson Associates.
Past performance does not guarantee future results.

# FIGURE 6.6

# S&P 500
## 1999
### The Entire Gain Occurred in Just 22 Weeks

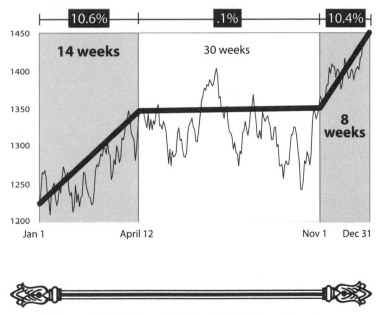

Performance of the S&P 500 Index from Jan. 1, 1999 through Dec. 31, 1999. Source: Ibbotson Associates.
Past performance does not guarantee future results.

# S&P 500
## 1998
### The Entire Gain Occurred in Just 11 Weeks

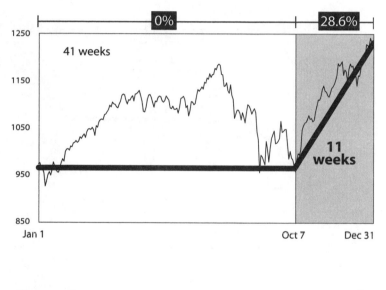

Performance of the S&P 500 Index from Jan. 1, 1998 through Dec. 31, 1998. Source: Ibbotson Associates.
Past performance does not guarantee future results.

FIGURE 6.8

# S&P 500
## 1997
### The Entire Gain Occurred in Just 15 Weeks

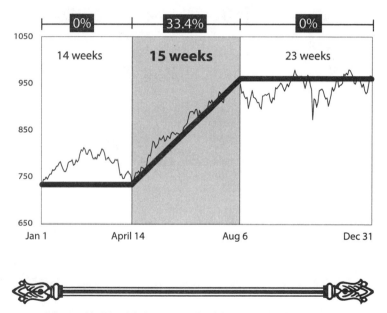

Performance of the S&P 500 Index from Jan. 1, 1997 through Dec. 31, 1997. Source: Ibbotson Associates. Past performance does not guarantee future results.

FIGURE 6.9

# S&P 500
## 1996
### The Entire Gain Occurred in Just 20 Weeks

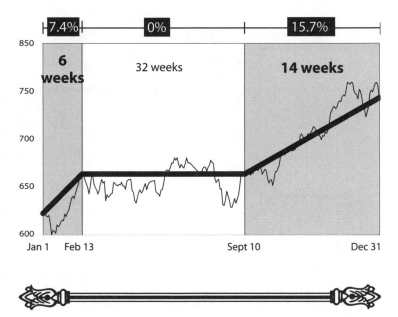

Performance of the S&P 500 Index from Jan. 1, 1996 through Dec. 31, 1996. Source: Ibbotson Associates.
Past performance does not guarantee future results.

FIGURE 6.10

# S&P 500
## 1992
### The Entire Gain Occurred in Just 6 Weeks

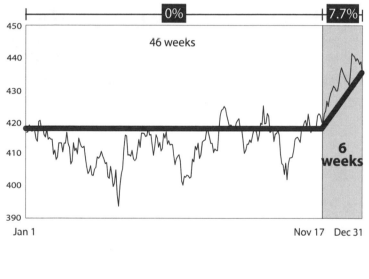

Performance of the S&P 500 Index from Jan. 1, 1992 through Dec. 31, 1992. Source: Ibbotson Associates.
Past performance does not guarantee future results.

# FIGURE 6.11

# S&P 500
## 1991
## The Entire Gain Occurred in Just 21 Weeks

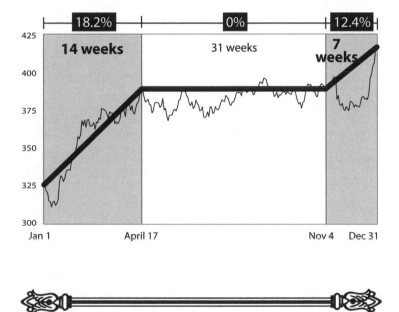

Performance of the S&P 500 Index from Jan. 1, 1991 through Dec. 31, 1991. Source: Ibbotson Associates.
Past performance does not guarantee future results.

In case you don't get the point, I will explain it.

It is common for the stock market to jump in short spurts that are followed by long periods of stagnation.

Can you predict when those short spurts are going to occur?

Me neither. That's why we remain invested the entire time, so we can catch the profits when they come.

Here's another real-world example:

If you were invested in the stock market from 1994 through 2008, you would have earned 6.5 percent per year over the market's 3,827 trading days,[22] as shown in Figure 6.12.

But if you missed the best ten days of that fifteen-year period, your average annual return would have been zero. The entire profit of fifteen years came in ten days.

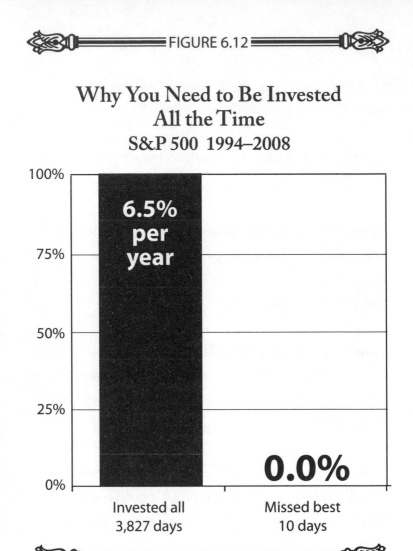

FIGURE 6.12

# Why You Need to Be Invested All the Time
## S&P 500  1994–2008

**6.5% per year**

**0.0%**

Invested all
3,827 days

Missed best
10 days

Source: Ibbotson Associates. Past performance does not guarantee future results.

Could you have picked the 10 days out of 3,827?

Do you think that some magazine columnist or television pundit can? You get the point.

In case you don't, I'll say it again: the only way you can be sure that you will capture the profits when they occur is to be invested the entire time. Thus, the first crucial step to achieving investment success through diversification is to maintain a long-term focus.

But how do you do that in the face of a difficult, downright scary economic environment?

You begin by remembering what history teaches us. We've experienced twelve recessions since 1945. The average stock market decline was 30 percent and lasted fifteen months, as shown in Figure 6.13. The longest (1946 to 49) lasted three years.[23]

More important, every recession has been followed by a tremendous bull market.

FIGURE 6.13

# S&P 500 During Bear Markets

|  | %<br>Return | #<br>Months |
| --- | --- | --- |
| May 29, 1946 – June 13, 1949 | –30% | 37 |
| Aug 2, 1956 – Oct 22, 1957 | –22% | 15 |
| Dec 12, 1961 – June 26, 1962 | –28% | 7 |
| Feb 9, 1966 – Oct 7, 1966 | –22% | 8 |
| Nov 29, 1968 – May 26, 1970 | –36% | 18 |
| Jan 11, 1973 – Oct 3, 1974 | –48% | 21 |
| Sept 21, 1976 – Mar 6, 1978 | –19% | 18 |
| Nov 28, 1980 – Aug 12, 1982 | –27% | 21 |
| Aug 25, 1987 – Dec 24, 1987 | –34% | 4 |
| July 16, 1990 – Oct 11, 1990 | –20% | 3 |
| July 17, 1998 – Aug 31, 1998 | –19% | 2 |
| Mar 24, 2000 – Oct 9, 2002 | –49% | 31 |
| **Average** | **–30%** | **15** |

Source: The Leuthold Group

On average, the S&P 500 has risen 38.1 percent in the first twelve months of the market's recovery.[24] Furthermore, in the last four recessions, stock prices began rising an average of four months before the recessions ended.[25]

Thus, investors who sell during a decline, thinking they'll wait for the economy to recover before investing again, are almost certain to miss much of the stock market's recovery.

Anyone who says it will take decades for the stock market to reach new highs simply doesn't know what he or she is talking about.

But what if this time is different?

People have been saying that for years. When the stock market crashed in 1987, many people said, "This time it's different."

People said it during the 1991 recession and the bear market between 2000 and 2002.

People also said it when prices were high. In 1999, when I warned on the radio that tech stocks were too high, investors said, "This time it's different." And in 2005, when I said that housing prices would not continue to rise, people said, "This time it's different."

No, it wasn't. And no, it isn't this time, either.

These times are not different, and the times to come won't be different, either.

Yet people insist that every period of extreme volatility is different.

It never proves true.

What is true about recessions, however, is that stock prices rise before the economy recovers. That's because investors can envision profits before they are actually earned. Still, you might ask, if economic weakness is in our short-term future, why not sell and move to cash and wait for the storm to end instead of risking your life savings further?

History provides the reason why you shouldn't do that: past recessions, panics, and depressions have taught us that stock markets recover with astonishing suddenness and velocity. By the time you realize that the bottom has been reached, prices have *already* risen sharply — meaning that you are forced to buy back in at prices that are higher than when you sold.

The key to succeeding with my advice, then, is patience. Another way to state this is that you should build your diversified portfolio — and then do nothing.

A fascinating study along these lines was published in the November 2007 *Journal of Economic Psychology.* Scientists examined the behavior of elite soccer goalkeepers during penalty kicks. Although that might seem off point, the study actually has important implications regarding your investment decisions.

Because the ball in a penalty kick takes only a few hundredths of a second to reach the goal line, the goalkeeper must decide *before* the ball is kicked whether to jump left, jump right, or stay in the middle. Since the study found that the ball is kicked to each of the three areas in equal proportions, you'd assume that goalies do each of the three in equal amounts.

But the researchers discovered that goalies stay in the center only 6.3 percent of the time.

That seems to make no sense. Why aren't goalies standing in the center more often?

The reason is simple. The goalie knows that he's likely to fail; indeed, 80 percent of the time, a goal is scored. So the fear is not that he'll fail — the fear is that he'll look stupid while failing.

Imagine that you're the goalie. You're standing on the goal line. The ball is kicked to the left or right 66 percent of the time — and you're just standing there. You know what everyone is thinking.

*Why didn't you <u>do</u> something?*

Thus, goalies figure that jumping to one side makes them look like they've tried. They feel that action is better than inaction — even though such action actually hurts their results.

The study's authors state, "The action/omission bias … has very important implications for economics and management. For example, the action/omission bias might affect the decision of investors whether to change their portfolio (action) or not (inaction)."

In other words, don't just do something, stand there!

The alternative is to buy and sell in a frenzy, without really knowing what you're doing or why you're doing it. Perhaps the time that Jim Cramer sold on Friday and bought on Tuesday is an example.

That's why, as I said, the first crucial step in achieving investment success through diversification is to maintain a long-term focus.

## *Crucial Step 2: Buy Low/Sell High*

The second crucial step to diversification is to engage in strategic rebalancing.

This step is vital if you're to achieve long-term success. Unfortunately, it's ignored by the overwhelming majority of investors.

The good news is that it's easy to understand and even easier to do.

To explain, let's begin with a sample portfolio. In this hypothetical example, we're going to invest equally in stocks, bonds, government securities, and cash, as shown in Figure 6.14.

# If This is the Portfolio We Want . . .

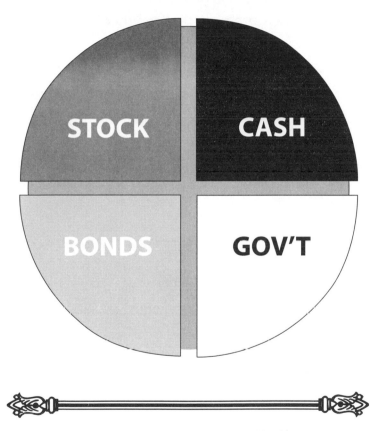

This is a hypothetical illustration to demonstrate the principle of diversification.
It is not representative of the past or future results of any specific investment.

Over time, one asset class will inevitably outperform the others.

Let's assume that stocks will be the outperforming investment. You see the results in Figure 6.15: stocks now represent a larger portion of our portfolio than before.

The portfolio is no longer balanced. This is a problem because our portfolio is not allocated the way we designed it. So, we must fix it.

We must rebalance the portfolio.

How?

Simple.

We sell.

Sell what?

We sell some stock.

FIGURE 6.15

## . . . Then We Need to Rebalance
## If the Portfolio Later Looks Like This

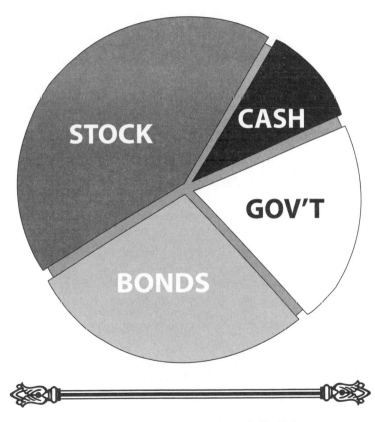

This is a hypothetical illustration to demonstrate the principle of diversification.
It is not representative of the past or future results of any specific investment.

And what do we do with that money?

We buy the asset class that now has too small a portion — in this case, the cash portion of our portfolio.

Thus, we sell some stock because we have too much of it. We buy some cash because we don't have enough. In other words, we sell the asset that made the most money and we buy the asset that made the least (or maybe even lost) money.

We sell the winner. We buy the loser.

Want me to say that again?

You're thinking that's crazy. Sell the investment that's made a lot of money? Buy the one that's losing money? Imagine coming home from work and saying to your spouse, "Hey, honey! You know that investment that made us a fortune? I just sold it. And you know that one where we lost our shirts? I bought more!"

At first glance, this doesn't seem to make sense — which explains why so few investors do it. But selling your winners and buying your losers is the smartest action you can take. It's counterintuitive, but it's the key to successful investing.

Remember that I promised to tell you how to buy low/sell high? Well, I just did.

Actually, I just told you to sell high/buy low. I reversed the phrase, which is why you stumbled over it. But whether you say buy low/sell high, or sell high/buy low, you get the same results.

You don't want to do it. Yet you wonder why you're not getting rich.

I'm simply telling you to buy when prices are low and sell when prices are high. You don't know how to do that because you don't know when the price is high or low. That's because you compare an investment's price to its former price and wonder what its future price will be.

I'm telling you not to do that. Instead compare an investment not to itself but to the other investments in your portfolio. When you do this, your portfolio will tell you what to do. No predictions are required. Your portfolio will automatically tell you that one asset is too high in price *relative to your other investments* (because it constitutes a larger portion of your overall portfolio) and that another asset is too low in price relative to your other investments.

It's obvious that you don't want to buy (or own) investments that are too high in price, and you do want to buy investments that are suddenly low in price (and, hence, a bargain).

As a consumer, you know this.

You know that the time to buy a big-screen TV is when it's on sale. Would you ever tell your spouse, "Sorry, but we can't buy that television now. It's on sale. We have to wait for the sale to be over, so we can buy it when the price is higher."

You go to the store to buy your favorite ice cream. You see that it's on sale. You don't buy the one gallon you intended to buy. You buy four.

Investors refuse to behave as intelligently. They want to buy only investments that have made a lot of money lately. If an investment isn't at an all-time high, they don't want it.

No one wants to buy gold at $200 an ounce. But when it reaches $1,000 an ounce, they load up. Later, when it falls to $700 and they've lost 30 percent, they sell and swear that never again will they buy gold.

The truth is simple: if you want to make money from investments, you must sell high/buy low. By *strategically rebalancing* (which is what this concept is called), you will spend your investment career selling assets that are higher in price than others and buying assets that are lower in price.

Sell high/buy low. You now know the secret to successful investing.

## The Penalty If You Fail to Buy Low/Sell High

I hope you can see the pitfall of failing to buy low/sell high.

In case you don't, I'll elaborate.

Some investors, seeing that some assets have grown in value while others have fallen (or, if their entire portfolio is down, as in 2008, and they see that some have fallen less than others), think that the smart action is to sell the loser and buy the winner. They want to get rid of the investment that's doing poorly and buy more of the asset that's doing better.

It's easy to fall into this trap. Media types encourage it by interviewing the fund managers who made a lot of money last year. They don't tell you that past performance does not guarantee future results.

Brokers encourage it too. They love to pitch five-star funds (and they don't tell you that the ratings change monthly).

Have you ever seen a broker recommend a one-star fund?

If you fall victim to this trap, you could experience the same trauma as the gentleman on page 71. Here's how that could happen.

Say you start out with a diversified portfolio. You then sell the assets that perform poorly and buy more of the asset that has performed well.

Eventually your portfolio might consist of only one asset — like the gentleman who held only stocks in his retirement account. He believed that was the best asset class because it *had been* the best asset class.

You need to avoid his mistake by selling out of asset classes and market sectors as they climb in value and buying more of asset classes and market sectors as they fall in value.

If you don't sell high/buy low, you'll wish you did.

### The Right Time to Buy Low/Sell High

You now realize the importance of rebalancing.

But when should you do it? There are two ways: time and percentage. Let's take a look.

### Rebalancing by Time

We don't rebalance our clients' portfolios this way, but it's easy, works relatively well, and is better than not rebalancing at all.

Simply rebalance on a calendar basis.

Many people rebalance quarterly. Many employer retirement plans and mutual fund companies will rebalance your account automatically upon request.

It's simple and painless, but not always as effective as you might like. Often, calendar rebalancing forces you to rebalance for no reason.

If you rebalance quarterly, you'll rebalance on June 30 whether the portfolio needs it or not. And you may often miss opportunities in between when rebalancing would be beneficial.

For instance, a short-term anomaly might cause an asset class to jump in price momentarily on April 12. A quick sale of high-priced assets and a purchase of low-cost assets would have locked in your gains. But calendar rebalancing will miss it.

Thus, rebalancing by time can cause you to rebalance when you don't need to and miss opportunities that don't coincide with your preset date.

### *Rebalancing by Percentage*

This explains why my firm doesn't rebalance our clients' portfolios according to the calendar. Instead we track each client's individual portfolio.

We begin by providing each client with his or her target asset allocation. For instance, we might designate that a client place 10 percent of his investments into a given asset class. We'll allow the value of that asset class to drift up or down within a certain range — perhaps as high as 12 percent or as low as 8 percent. But if the asset's holdings cross either threshold, a rebalance will occur.

Thus, we rebalance only and whenever it is needed.

The problem with rebalancing by percentage is that we never know when an asset is about to cross its threshold. We solve that problem by monitoring each client's account every day.

That might sound cumbersome, which may explain why most consumers don't do it for themselves. It may also be one reason why consumers choose to hire us. They know that rebalancing is important, but it's also a chore. So they happily delegate the task to us.

Normally, a properly designed portfolio will need to be rebalanced only one to four times per year. But in unusual markets, such as those we experienced in 2008, we found ourselves rebalancing a dozen times or more for many clients.

By executing rebalances when needed, you can reduce your portfolio's volatility, reduce your investment risks, and improve your returns.

So, rebalance.

Do it by time or do it by percentage. But do it.

# *What If You're Already Retired?*

If you're already retired, you're shaking your head.

Sure, I've told you some great things about diversification and long-term investing. But you don't have a long term to invest.

If you are already retired or about to be, your perspective is not the same as people in their twenties, thirties, forties, or fifties.

But what you've read offers lessons for you as well.

Too often people in or near retirement place all their money into bank accounts. As we've seen, they fear risk, need safety, and want income. So they put their money into CDs, bonds, and U.S. Treasuries, and they spend the income those investments generate.

That's a problem. A big problem. But it takes years for people to realize that.

Consider the interest rate on a one-year CD. If you invested $100,000 into that CD in 1990, you would have earned $6,800 in interest.[26] But in 2009, you would need $10,441 to buy the same goods and services due to 2.9 average annual inflation during that period.[27]

Yet one-year CDs in January 2009 were paying just $2,530.[28]

That's scary.

This is the challenge that retirees face. They need income now. They also need income in the future. Thus, it's not enough for the current principal to generate income. The principal must also rise so that it can generate more income in the future to offset inflation.

We face this problem daily in my firm because about 40 percent of our clients are retired. So we devote substantial amounts of effort to helping thousands of people live comfortably on their life savings.

Our solution for them is called a systematic withdrawal plan.

This strategy offers our clients the opportunity to generate not only current income but an increased income that keeps pace with inflation and the cost of living.

Too often retirees emphasize their need for current income without regard for their future needs. Don't make this mistake.

Don't let your parents make this mistake.

Don't let your grandparents make this mistake.

Don't place life savings into low-yielding accounts where the principal balance can't grow. Instead place it into a diversified portfolio and use it to generate the income you need.

134   Rescue Your Money

# *The Most Important Part of the Secret*

So the secret is out. Diversification.

You get it. You agree with it. And you already do it.

Or at least you think you do.

People often tell me they are diversified. They brag that they own ten — count 'em, *ten* — mutual funds.

*"It ain't so much the things we don't know that get us in trouble. It's the things we know that ain't so."*

*— Artemus Ward*

A fellow once showed me his account statements. He was very proud of himself because he had *eighty* mutual funds. He told me that he was "highly diversified." (I wrote about him in *Discover the Wealth Within You.*)

A close look revealed that he owned eight money market funds, twenty-three government bond funds, and forty-nine U.S. stock funds. But not a single foreign stock fund. No real estate. No gold. No oil.

Forty-nine stock funds? Every one of them owned shares of Microsoft!

He wasn't diversified.

He was redundant.

Let me show you what diversification really looks like. Look at Figure 8.1.

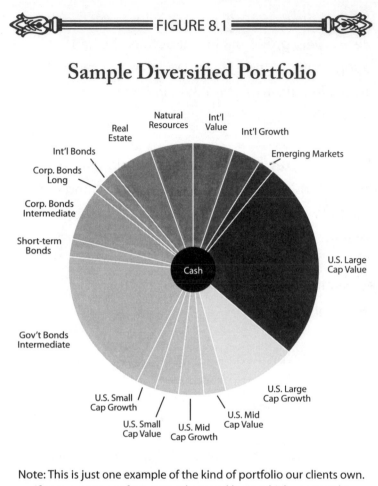

## FIGURE 8.1

# Sample Diversified Portfolio

Note: This is just one example of the kind of portfolio our clients own. If you want to see forty-two others and learn which one is right for you, read *The Lies About Money*.

A truly diversified portfolio will own U.S. stocks: large cap, mid cap, and small cap, broken down by growth and value sectors.

It will own foreign stocks, including emerging markets.

It will own bonds, both government and corporate, each including short-term, intermediate, and long-term, and — for the corporate portion — high-quality and high-yield.

It will own real estate: commercial, residential, retail, industrial, and agricultural, all geographically dispersed.

It will own natural resources, including oil and gas, precious metals, and commodities.

A truly diversified portfolio will own it all, all the time!

Anyway, that's how we do it in my firm's practice. Our clients typically invest in nineteen separate asset classes and market sectors.

We minimize redundancy. For example, our clients typically own upwards of ten thousand stocks from forty countries.

And they do it by owning from four to twenty-two funds.

Surprised that we don't buy individual stocks and bonds? Too risky for us. Too risky for our clients.

For the ten years preceding December 31, 2008, as shown in Figure 8.2, only 42 percent of all stocks listed on the New York Stock Exchange made money.[29]

During that same period, 56 percent of mutual funds made money.[30]

And as Figure 8.3 shows, the average fund grew 9.4 percent during this period,[31] while the average stock *fell* 7.8 percent.[32]

The reason funds have lower risks and higher returns is simple.

Funds are diversified.

Even the worst of them own two dozen securities, while the best own thousands.

That's why we invest in funds for our clients.

Simple.

Easy.

And you can do it too.

But we don't use retail mutual funds for the Edelman Managed Asset Program®.

Instead, my firm recommends exchange-traded funds and institutional shares for our clients.

It wasn't always this way.

# Portion That Were Profitable
## 1999–2008

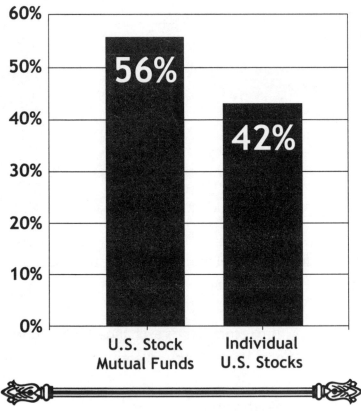

Sources: Morningstar. Past performance does not guarantee future results.

FIGURE 8.3

# Average Cumulative Total Return
## 1999–2008

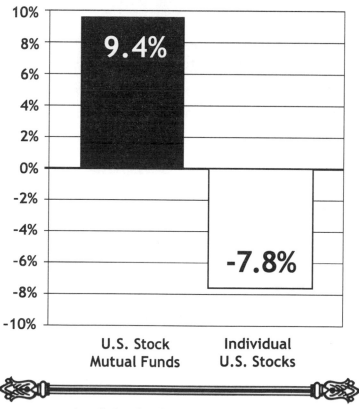

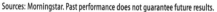

Sources: Morningstar. Past performance does not guarantee future results.

In years past, we used to recommend traditional retail mutual funds. Why we don't, and how we went about making the conversion, is explained in great detail in *The Lies About Money,* which won the Gold Medal for Personal Finance in 2008 from the Axiom Business Book Awards.

In *Lies,* I reveal twenty-five deceptive business practices used by the mutual fund industry. To help you avoid having to read another book, here are two of the more onerous business practices mutual funds use, which cause investors to incur greater risk, higher fees, and lower returns than you realize.

### *Turnover*

Turnover is the enemy of long-term investors. The average stock mutual fund experiences 80 percent turnover annually.[33] In other words, 80 percent of the assets owned by the fund on January 1 are sold during the year and replaced with new assets.

It's ironic. You probably consider yourself to be a long-term investor. But if your mutual fund is flipping 80 percent of your assets annually, you're not really a long-term investor. Your fund has converted you into a short-term trader!

All that trading forces you to pay more taxes. That's because trading triggers short-term capital gains, which you must pay at your maximum tax rate. It will come in the way of the IRS Form 1099 that you will receive from your retail mutual fund company. This form shows taxable distributions that the fund has made during the year.

Remember how volatile the markets were in 2008? Amidst that volatility, many managers of retail mutual funds were buying and selling lots of securities for their funds. When a fund sells a security, the sale generates a realized capital gain (or loss). If the stock sold had been purchased less than a year ago, the trades are classified as short-term. Net gains are distributed by year-end, meaning that investors receive a Form 1099 requiring them to pay as much as 40 percent in federal and state income taxes. And the capital gains distributions are taxable even if you reinvest the distribution back into the fund.

In 2008 many retail mutual funds made distributions equal to 20 percent or more of their assets. Anyone who had $100,000 in such a fund could have incurred $7,000 or more in taxes.

And that's not all.

### *Fees*

All that trading also increases your costs.

After all, someone has to pay the brokerage commissions when your fund buys or sells a security. This is one reason why investors of retail mutual funds pay high fees.

Yet, amazingly, most consumers think that they don't pay any fees to own their mutual funds. That's what AARP discovered in 2007 when it surveyed workers around the country. An astonishing 65 percent said they don't pay any fees to own their mutual funds.

Who do they think is paying for the fund company to issue statements and provide toll-free telephone numbers and staff to answer those phone calls? Clearly there are fees involved. It's just that the fees aren't obvious.

They aren't obvious because they aren't on your statement.

If your bank charges you a fee, that fee appears on your statement. When you buy a car, you know how much you're paying. Even your mortgage statement shows you how much of your payment is going toward interest on the loan.

But mutual fund fees don't appear on your statement. The statement shows only the number of shares you own and the share price.

But never the fee.

It's no wonder that so many consumers think they aren't paying anything to own their mutual funds.

Of course there is a fee. It's called the annual expense ratio, and the average annual expense ratio for all retail mutual funds is 1.23 percent per year.[34]

But don't look for this information on your statement; it isn't there. You'll have to read the prospectus to find it.

The expense ratio covers the routine costs of fund operations: staff, facilities, marketing, and so on. It does not include the costs of trading. *That* expense is found in another document called the statement of additional information. The average retail mutual fund charges 1.44 percent annually in trading expenses.[35]

In all, you're paying the average retail mutual fund 2.67 percent per year. Based on the stock market's average annual return of 9.6 percent a year,[36] that means you're giving away 28 percent of your profits on an annual basis.

Imagine giving a waiter a 28 percent tip.

This might explain why so many members of the Forbes 400 (the wealthiest people in America) are the founders or owners of big mutual fund companies.

Ned and Abby Johnson, whose family owns Fidelity Investments, are worth $26 billion, according to the 2008 *Forbes* list.

Charlie and Rupert Johnson (no relation to Ned and Abby) are worth $9 billion. They own the Franklin Templeton mutual fund family.

John Calamos of Calamos Investments and Bill Gross of Pimco are each worth nearly $2 billion.

Michael Price sold the Mutual Series fund family to Franklin; he's now worth $1.7 billion.

Tom Marsico of Marsico Funds is worth $1.5 billion.

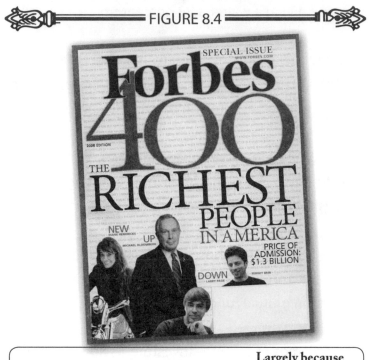

| Name | Are Worth | Largely because of an ownership stake in: |
|------|-----------|------------------------------------------|
| Ned and Abby Johnson | $26 Billion | Fidelity |
| Johnson Brothers | $9 Billion | Franklin |
| John Calamos | $2 Billion | Calamos |
| Bill Gross | $2 Billion | Pimco |
| Michael Price | $1.7 Billion | Mutual Series |
| Tom Marsico | $1.5 Billion | Marsico |

The U.S. retail mutual fund industry is a $9.4 trillion industry.[37] Collectively, U.S. equity and bond mutual funds charge $248 billion in fees each year. No wonder these guys are among the wealthiest people in America.

Turnover and fees are just two of the twenty-five deceptive business practices used by the retail mutual fund industry. That's why we say no to them.

Instead we use institutional mutual funds and exchange-traded funds. Most folks are unaware of these investments, yet they represent the solution to the deceptive and manipulative business practices of the retail mutual fund world.

Now, you might be a little confused. I just told you to say no to retail mutual funds, and now I'm recommending institutional mutual funds. Let me explain the difference.

An institutional fund is typically marketed to institutions and often requires you to invest millions of dollars. That's why you've never heard of them. As a retail investor working with a retail advisor at a retail brokerage firm, you don't have access to them.

You see, others with billions of dollars to invest approach the investment decision differently from those of us who have, say, smaller amounts of money.

Here's what I mean. Imagine I give $1,000 to you and another $1,000 to your friend. I send you both into Wal-Mart with only one instruction: you must both spend all the money. Will you and your friend emerge with the same merchandise?

With more than 142,000 items in the store,[38] probably not.

So let's change the rules. I send you both back into the store. But this time you each get $1 billion. Now will you both emerge with the same merchandise?

You certainly will.

After all, with $1 billion at your disposal, it's no longer a question of what to buy. You have no choice but to buy everything.

This is the dilemma faced by David Swensen. He's the manager of the Yale Endowment Fund, a $17 billion portfolio.[39]

He doesn't have the luxury of deciding whether to buy Coca-Cola or Pepsi. With $17 billion to spend, he must buy both.

Thus, for the David Swensens of the financial world, the decision is not which stock to buy but how much money to put into stocks in the first place — as opposed to bonds, real estate, gold, or oil and gas.

For David Swensen, what matters is the asset allocation question.

As a result, institutional funds are very consistent in their holdings.

They engage in little turnover because there's nothing left to buy. That means expenses are lower, and so is the annual tax liability for shareholders.

There are other cost savings too. If you're going to buy everything, you don't need a high-priced portfolio manager backed by a team of security analysts. All you need is a clerk to handle the transactions.

Although many institutional funds are not available to retail investors like you, some are. For example, my firm provides the funds of Dimensional Fund Advisors to our clients. Another thousand or so other financial advisors also have this ability.

But there's another way to enjoy a market-based (rather than manager-based) investment approach. They're called exchange-traded funds, and my firm provides these to our clients in addition to institutional funds.

ETFs have been around since 1993. Like institutional funds, they're up to 90 percent cheaper than the average retail mutual fund. ETFs trade on the New York Stock Exchange. This means that you can buy them from any discount brokerage firm: TD Ameritrade, E*Trade Financial, Charles Schwab & Co., you name it.

Because ETFs trade via brokerage accounts, they cost much less to operate. They pass the savings to you.

# *Conclusion*

So now you know the secret to successful investing. Build a highly diversified portfolio consisting of low-cost institutional shares and exchange-traded funds. Buy low/sell high through strategic rebalancing, and maintain a long-term investment horizon.

That's all there is to it.

If you prefer, you can do this yourself with any discount broker. If you wish, you can retain a financial advisor to handle it for you.

Which is the better approach?

Well, if you know how to construct a portfolio and research investments for it, you might consider doing it yourself. You'll need to monitor the portfolio to execute rebalances as needed, and you'll have to handle your own paperwork and record keeping for tax purposes.

If you prefer not to spend your time on all that, consider delegating these chores to an advisor. That pretty much describes the kind of people who hire my firm and firms like us. They know that they need a proper investment strategy, but they don't want to have to do it themselves. By turning to a firm like mine, someone will handle everything for you.

Other firms provide similar services. So the choice is yours. Do it yourself or hire someone to do it for you.

But do it.

And remember back in chapter 1 when I told you about the one major investment goal you should have?

That goal, if you recall, is financial security.

The best way to achieve it is to generate above-average returns with below-average risks and below-average costs.

If you follow the advice outlined in this book, you'll be well on your way to achieving the financial security you want for yourself and your family.

# Ric's Recipe

Prep time: the long-term (at least 5 years)

Serves: your entire family with heaping
portions of financial security

### What You'll Need:

1 Cup of Media Advice

1 Pinch of Investment Fads

1 Cup of High-Cost Mutual Funds

1 Dash of Blue-Chip Stocks

2 Teaspoons of ETFs

1 Tablespoon of Institutional Shares

Take a knife to your high-cost retail mutual funds and chop them into little pieces. Repeat with the media advice, investment fads, and blue-chip stocks. Combine with the chopped funds and discard.

In a clean pan, combine ETFs with institutional shares. Cover and let simmer for a long time. Rebalance periodically. At retirement, enjoy!

Illustration by Wendy Sefcik

160

# *Notes*

1. Standard & Poor's.

2. Consumer Price Index for All Urban Consumers: All Items Year-over-Year Change — Data Series Monthly January 1926–November 2007. Source: Bureau of Labor Statistics.

3. TrimTabs Investment Research.

4. *Extraordinary Popular Delusions and the Madness of Crowds* by Charles Mackay. Published in 1852.

5. Investopedia.

6. Dow Jones & Company.

7. Bloomberg.

8. NASDAQ (National Association of Securities Dealers Automated Quotations).

9. Standard & Poor's.

10. NASDAQ; Ibbotson Associates.

11. S&P/Case-Shiller Composite Home Index and National Association of Realtors.

12. Dow Jones & Company.

13. *Fortune*; Standard & Poor's.

14. Case Western Reserve University, 2000.

15. DuPont.

16. Of the 500 stocks in the S&P 500 on January 1, 2000, only 353 were still in the index on December 31, 2008. The rest were delisted, acquired by other firms or out of business. Of the 353, 49 percent ended 2008 with lower market values than they had on January 1, 2000. Source: Bloomberg.

17. Employee Benefit Research Institute.

18. Ibbotson Associates.

19. Ibbotson Associates.

20. Ibbotson Associates.

21. Ibbotson Associates.

22. Ibbotson Associates.

23. The Leuthold Group.

24. Ibbotson Associates.

25. National Bureau of Economic Research.

26. Ibbotson Associates.

27. Ibbotson Associates.

28. The average one-year CD rate according to Bankrate.com as of January 10, 2009.

29. Bloomberg.

30. Morningstar.

31. Bloomberg.

32. Morningstar.

33. Morningstar.

34. Morningstar.

35. 2007 study by the Virginia Polytechnic Institute and State University, the University of Virginia, and Boston College.

36. Performance of the S&P 500, 1926–2008, according to Ibbotson Associates.

37. Investment Company Institute.

38. Wal-Mart.

39. Yale University.

# *Index*

Note: Boldface page numbers refer to figures.

advice
  expert, 42–44
  from media, 28, 37–42, 82–85
advisors, financial, 157–58
AIG, 41
airline industry, 50
American Association of Retired
    People (AARP), 146–47
asset allocation, **117**, **119**, 128, 153
asset class
  and buy low/sell high, 116, 118,
    120–23
  and diversification, 77, **78–79**, 80,
    **138**, 140
  and failure to buy low/sell high, 125
  and returns, 24, **25**, **78–79**
Axiom Business Book Awards, 144

Bank of America, 41
*Barron's*, 39
Beanie Babies, 32
bear markets, **57**, **110**, 112
beating the market, as goal of
    investors, 7–9
best-known companies, quality of,
    45, **46**, 47–49
bonds, 24, **25**, **79**, 85, **86**, 116, **117**,
    **119**, **138**, 139, 140, 153
Boston College, 148, 163
Buffett, Warren, 83
bull markets, **57**, 109
Bunker, Nelson and William, 32
buy low/sell high
  and asset class, 116, 118, 120–23
  and diversification, 116, **117**, 118,

**119**, 120–23
  importance of, 116, 118, 120–23
  and market timing, 28, **30**
  penalty for failure to, 124–25
  returns when, 27
  as secret of successful investing,
    **4**, 5
  and "truths" about successful
    investing, 65
  *See also* timing, market
buying power. *See* inflation

Calamos Funds, 149, **150**
Calamos, John, 149, **150**
calendar rebalancing, 126–27
capital gains taxes, **13**, 145–46
Case Western Reserve University, 162
cautionary tale, 69–72, **73**, 125
CDs (certificate of deposits), 16–17,
    **18**, 20, **25**, 132
Charles Schwab & Co., 155
CNBC, 39, 62
Coca-Cola, **46**, 153
Cramer, Jim, 39–40, 84, 115
crash of 1987, 111

Dimensional Fund Advisors, 154
diversification
  and asset class, 77, **78–79**, 80, **138**,
    140
  and buy low/sell high, 116, **117**,
    118, **119**, 120–23
  example of, **138**, 139
  and long-term focus, 109, 112–15
  and mutual funds, 135, 137, 141

diversification (cont.)
  and retirement, 134
  and returns, 80
  and risk, 84–86, 93
  as secret of investing, 77–91, 135, 157
  and sectors, 77, **81**, **138**, 139, 140
  and volatility, 85, **86**
Dow Jones Industrial Average
  annual rate of return over time
    of, 69
  and beating the market, 7
  and cautionary tale, 70, 71
  in future, 66, 68
  and market timing, 29
  and media, 37, 38, 40
  yearly averages of, 66, **67**, 68
DuPont, 45, **46**

E*Trade Financial, 155
economic recovery, and price,
  111–12
Edelman Managed Asset Program®,
  141
employers, buying stock of, 48–49
Enron, 48
exchange-traded funds (ETFs), 141,
  151, 154–55, 157
expense ratio, 148, 154
experts, advice from, 42–44, 82–83

fads, 31–34, **35**, 36, 65
Fannie Mae, 40–41, **46**
fees, for mutual funds, 144, 146–49,
  151–54
Fidelity Investments, 149, **150**
financial advisors, 154, 157–58
financial security, as goal of
  investors, 8–9, 11, 159
*Forbes* magazine
  400 richest people listed in, 149, **150**

  Hess advice in, 40–41
foreign stocks, 34, 50, **54**, **78**, 85,
  137, **138**, 139
*Fortune* magazine, 38, 41, 82, 162
Franklin, Benjamin, 2
Franklin Templeton, 149, **150**
Freddie Mac, 40–41, **46**

General Electric, **46**, 47
goal, financial security as, 8–9, 159
goals, important, 7–9
Goodman, George, 91
Gross, Bill, 149, **150**
growth stocks, as hot sector, 50,
  51, **52**

Hess, Lisa, 40–41
Hewitt Associates, 49
Hewlett-Packard, **46**, 47
Honeywell International, **46**, 47
hot sectors, 50–51, **52–54**, 65
housing, 112
Hunt brothers, 33, **35**

Ibbotson Associates, **25**, **30**, **35**, **52–
  54**, **57**, **61**, **63**, **67**, **81**, **86**, **88**, **95**,
  **97–106**, **108**, **162–63**
IBM, **46**, 47
individual stocks, 140, **142–43**
inflation
  effect of, **18**
  as fact of life, **15**
  as obstacle to investing, 11–12, **13**,
    **15**, 16–17, **18**, 19–21
  and retirement, 133
institutional investors, 153
institutional mutual funds, 151–54,
  157
Internal Revenue Service (IRS), 14
Internet mania, 33, 34, **35**

Investment Company Institute, 29, **30**, 163

Japan, stock market in, 33, **35**
Johnson, Abby, 149, **150**
Johnson, Charlie, 149, **150**
Johnson, Ned, 149, **150**
Johnson, Rupert, 149, **150**
*Journal of Economic Psychology*, 113
  soccer study in, 113–15
JPMorgan Chase & Co., **46**, 47

large stocks, as hot sector, 50, 51, **53**
Leuthold Group, The, 110, 163
long-term focus
  and diversification, 109, 112–15
  and gains in Standard & Poor's 500
    index, 94, **95**, 96, **97–106**, **108**, 111
  importance of, 94, 96, 107, 109,
    111–15
  as secret of investing, 157
  and volatility and risk, 62, 64

McDonald's, **46**, 47, 49
market, beating the, 7–9, *See also*
  timing, market
Marsico Funds, 149, **150**
Marsico, Tom, 149, **150**
maximizing, 87, 89–90
media
  advice from, 28, 37–42, 65, 82–85
  and failure to buy low/sell high, 124
  and investing as horse race, 82–83
  not listening to, 65
  trusting the, 37–42
  and "truths" about successful
    investing, 62, 65
  and what the media never tells
    you, 83–85, 87
Merrill Lynch, 41, **46**

Microsoft, 137
*Money* magazine, 37, 38, 42, 82, 84
Morningstar, **142–43**, 163
mutual funds
  annual expense ratio for, 148
  deceptive business practices with
    retail, 144–49, 151–54
  and diversification, 135, 137, 141
  and expense ratio, 154
  expense ratio for, 148, 154
  fees for, 146–49, 151–55
  institutional, 151–54, 157
  retail, 141, 144
  and returns, 141
  returns from, **142**, **143**
  and risk, 141
  and taxes, 145–46, 154
  turnover in, 144–46, 151, 154
Mutual Series Funds, 149

NASDAQ, 33
National Bureau of Economic
  Research, 163
natural resources, and
  diversification, **138**, 139
New York Stock Exchange, 140, 155

*The Oprah Winfrey Show*, 48
optimizing, 87, 89–90

Pepsi, 153
percentage rebalancing, 127–29
Pimco, 149, **150**
Price, Michael, 149, **150**
price
  and economic recovery, 112–13
  and goal of investing, 159
  rise and fall of, 56, **57**, 58–59, 64–65
  and "truths" about investing, 56,
    **57**, 58–59

price (cont.)
  *See also* buy low/sell high

quality
  and best-known companies, **46**
  counting on, 45, 47–49
  and "truths" about investing, 65

real estate
  and diversification, **138**, 139
  as fad, 33, 34, **35**
  returns from, 24, **25**
rebalancing, 118, **119**, 123, 126–29,
  158
recession, 109, **110**, 112–13
retail mutual funds, 141, 144–49,
  151–54
retirement, 131–34
return, and goal of investing, 159
returns
  and asset class, 24, **25**
  average annual, **88**
  and buy low/sell high, 27
  and diversification, 80
  and hot sectors, 51
  from individual stocks, **142**, **143**
  minimum, 21, **22**, 23
  from mutual funds, 141, **142**, **143**
  and obstacles to investing, 16–17,
    **18**, 19–20, 21, **22**, 23, 24, **25**
  and rebalancing, 128
  risk versus, 84–86, 89
  and "safe" investments, 16–17, **18**,
    19–20, 21, **22**, 23, 24, **25**
  that generate what you need,
    23–24, **25**
  and volatility, 89
  *See also* Dow Jones Industrial
    Average; Standard & Poor's 500
    index

richest people, *Forbes* list of, 149,
  **150**
risk
  and diversification, 84–86, 93
  fear of, 132
  and goal of investing, 159
  and hot sectors, 51
  and individual stocks and bonds,
    140
  and media predictions, 83–85
  and mutual funds, 141
  and obstacles to investing, 17
  and optimizing, 89
  and rebalancing, 128
  and retirement, 132
  returns versus, 84–86, 89
  stock market as too risky, 17
  and "truths" about investing, 60,
    **61**, 62–64
  and volatility, 89
Roaring Twenties, 32, **35**

"safe" investments
  and obstacles to investing, 16–17,
    **18**, 19–20, 21, 23, **25**
  and retirement, 132
secret
  most important part of, 135–55
  secret to the, 93–129
  of successful investing, 1–6
  what is the, 75–91, 157–59
sectors, market
  and diversification, 77, **81**, **138**,
    139
  hot, 50–51, **52**, 53–54
  investments in 14 versus 16, **81**
sell high/buy low. *See* buy low/sell
  high
silver, Hunt brothers attempt to
  corner, 33, **35**

small-cap stocks, as hot sector, 50, 51, **53**
South Sea Bubble, 32, **35**
Standard & Poor's 500 index
  bear markets in, **57**, **110**
  and beating the market, 7, 8
  bull markets in, **57**
  and Cramer's recommendations, 39
  and long-term focus, 94, **95**, 96, **97–106**, **108**, 111
  monthly performance from, 28–29, 60, **61**
  and obstacles to investing, 17
  and quality stocks, 47
  10-year performance of, 62, **63**
stocks
  individual, 140, **142–43**
  returns from, versus mutual funds, **142**, **143**
Swensen, David, 153

taxes
  effect of, **18**
  and mutual funds, 145–46, 154
  as obstacle to investing, 11–12, 16, **18**, 21
  recordkeeping for, 158
  top rates for, **13**
TD Ameritrade, 155
technology stocks, 31, 33, 34, **35**, 112
timing, market
  and fads, 31–34, **35**, 36
  and questions about investing, 28–29, **30**, 31
  and secret of successful investing, 116, 118, 120–23
  and time to buy low/sell high, 126

*See also* buy low/sell high
Trennert, Jason, 43
"truths"
  cautionary tale about, 69–73
  and price, 56–59
  and risk and volatility, 60–64
  that prevent successful investing, 55–73
  truth about, 65–68
Tulip Craze, 32, **35**
turnover, in mutual fund portfolios, 144–46, 151, 154

University of Virginia, 163
*U.S. News & World Report*, 37, 82
U.S. stocks
  foreign stocks versus, **54**
  as hot sector, 50, 51
  returns from, 24, **25**, **54**
*USA Today*, 38, 43, 82

value stocks, as hot sector, 50–51, **52**
Virginia Institute of Technology, 163
volatility
  and diversification, 85, **86**
  between 1972 and 1992, **86**
  and rebalancing, 128
  and returns, 89
  and risk, 89
  and "truths" about investing, 60, **61**, 62, **63**, 64–65
  and turnover in mutual fund portfolios, 144–46

Walt Disney Company, **46**, 47
withdrawal plan, retirement, 133–34

Yale Endowment Fund, 153

# More from Ric Edelman

**Talk to Ric Live at
888-PLAN-RIC**

## Tune In Nationwide to Ric's Radio Show

Every week, Ric gives you the information you need to help increase your wealth. Tune in for the answers about debt, mort-gages, college, insurance, choosing a financial advisor, estate planning, and more. Visit RicEdelman.com for local airtimes.

## Subscribe to Ric's Award-Winning Monthly Newsletter, *Inside Personal Finance*

You'll get the latest on personal finance delivered straight to your home every month. It's all explained in plain English, with Ric's unique perspective.

*Order online at RicEdelman.com
or call toll-free 888-987-7526.*

## Explore RicEdelman.com

Ric offers you free educational resources — articles, audio, video — all at RicEdelman.com.

## Also available in bookstores everywhere

Ric Edelman is an Investment Advisor Representative and offers advisory services through Edelman Financial Advisors LLC and Edelman Financial Services LLC, SEC regis-tered investment advisers. Ric is also a Registered Representative of and offers securities for Edelman Financial Services LLC through SMH Capital Inc., an independent broker/dealer, member FINRA/SIPC.

# About the Author

### Acclaimed Financial Advisor
Inducted into the Financial Advisor Hall of Fame in 2004, Ric has also been named by *Barron's* as one of America's 100 top financial advisors five times (2004–2008). With billions of dollars under management, Edelman Financial is one of the nation's largest advisory firms, serving thousands of consumers nationwide.

### Bestselling Author, Radio and TV Host, and Educator
Ric is a No. 1 *New York Times* bestselling author whose books have been translated into several languages worldwide. He hosts popular specials for PBS television and has appeared on *The Oprah Winfrey Show* five times.

*The Ric Edelman Show* has been airing for eighteen years and can be heard each weekend on radio stations throughout the country via the ABC Radio Networks.

Ric's advice column appears weekly in newspapers around the country. He also publishes a monthly newsletter, offers video and audio educational programs, and offers free information about personal finance at RicEdelman.com.

### Philanthropic Activities
Ric and Jean Edelman are major supporters of the Edelman Planetarium at Rowan University and the Edelman Nursing Career Development Center at the Inova Health System. Through donations and service as board members and volunteers, they support many other charities and nonprofit organizations, including the Boys & Girls Clubs of America, American Savings Education Council, and the Jump$tart Coalition for Personal Financial Literacy.